SUMMER AT THE RESORT

Remembering the Fifties

To Jockie
Central Park day were great.
Hope you enjoy the read.

Best Wishes ✿

Grady 8/21/98

Henry Grady Starnes

Cover design by
Leon Sears

Published by
Henry Grady Starnes

Distributed by:
Henry Grady Starnes
1039 Rowland Road
Stone Mountain,
Georgia 30083

ISBN: 0-9657613-0-4

Affiliated Lithographers
3128 West Thomas Rd.
Suite 201
Phoenix, Arizona 85017

About the Author

Grady Starnes grew up in the Atlanta area during the Depression of the 1930's. With the onset of World War II, his family moved to Savannah where his father had worked in the shipyards in World War I and again took up his trade as a ship carpenter. After his graduation from Savannah High School in 1949, Grady attended Piedmont College on an athletic scholarship and earned a degree in English in 1953. After serving two years in the Army and then beginning a teaching career, he earned an MA degree in English from Peabody Teacher's College in 1959.

In 1961 he joined a school textbook publishing company and traveled the country extensively as a representative and consultant. In this capacity, he says, he met the world and all of its characters. He later returned to teaching and is now writing about these experiences.

He married Ann Hawkins, also a graduate of Piedmont College, in 1953. They have been married for 43 years and have a son and daughter.

To Jesse

I first met Jesse Hill Ford at a writer's workshop in 1985 at Vanderbilt University of Nashville, Tennessee. Jesse and I braved Nashville's scorching summer heat several times to play tennis and became good friends. He was the teacher of writing, I of tennis and endurance.

The most important thing I learned from Jesse was that you can dream and talk about writing, but can only learn to write by making yourself do it. For his patience, criticism, and encouragement, I am deeply indebted.

ACKNOWLEDGMENT

Just about everybody I know wants to write a book, but few find the time and energy. For those of us who bare our souls, there are those who can find fault with our work but only a fraction who could match our efforts.

At a Savannah High School class reunion in 1989, I ran across my old friend and tennis partner Bobby Epps. Bobby had been living in California for 30 years and had recently retired as a technical editor for a research company.

He was quite interested in my writing and volunteered to edit the book for me. After his first reading, he advised me that my story had a lot of insignificant detail but also some very good writing. Bobby's encouragement and editing skills have made printing this book possible. His wife Willie proved to be an excellent reader and critic, and made invaluable suggestions.

❀ *Prologue*

I'm standing on the steps of a reinforced bunker on a freezing night in North Korea. Just over a year ago I was driving through the New England countryside with Yvonne when I heard a special announcement on the radio that U. S. forces under General MacArthur had invaded North Korea and had cut off the enemy and would destroy them. Military experts and politicians were saying that the war was won and our boys would be home by Christmas.

The car was dark, the music was soft, and the lovely Yvonne, mellow from wine, made everything seem perfect.

How far away that all seems now. Rand was killed on the Chinese border when China's huge "volunteer army" poured across the Yalu River and overran our forces. J.T. was wounded and sent back to the States, and I'm not sure what will happen to me if today is like yesterday. We are dug in with a river behind us and no chance of escape or being reinforced. The enemy dead are piled where they were killed in a fanatical attack on our position.

As I try to sort out our situation, my mind keeps returning to my college years and the summer at the resort. I can only recall how easy life was and what good times the three of us had. The frustrations of trying to make out with the girls, and the sometimes heart-wrenching romances, have receded behind the more pleasant memories.

It's dawn, the bugles blast away signaling a new attach, and in the distance the voices of thousands of screaming Chinese soldiers dedicated to final victory. A new day of killing has begun. God, what I would give to be out of here and back at the summer resort.

Chapter One

❀ *Walaholla to Points North*

There was a time when I was young and somewhat innocent. As a teenager in the late 1940's I believed that we Americans were the good guys and that everyone loved us, the nation that had saved the world from the tyrants of World War II.

The events I'm about to relate occurred during my final innocent years, in the early 1950's. The Korean War was underway, though known at the time as a "police action." Unlike World War II, still fresh in my memory, no one I knew wanted to volunteer for this one. Those of us in college were hoping that the war would end while we were still protected by our educational deferment.

I'm Claxton Carter from Savannah, Georgia. As this story opens I'm a freshman at Coyee College in Walaholla, South Carolina, which I'm attending on a sports scholarship (basketball and baseball mostly, with a little tennis on the side). As my freshman year drew to a close, it became time to figure out what I was going to do during the summer. My roommate Rand Cuthbert and I had played basketball and baseball together, and decided we might as well team up again on summer employment. We had no specific ideas, except that I knew I wasn't going to repeat last summer's punishing experience of pushing concrete in a wheelbarrow, even if construction work paid twice as much as most other temporary jobs.

One interesting prospect was working in a New England summer resort. I had found out about that from a friend in Savannah, who had worked at Handover, one of the many resorts in the Berkshire Mountains of western Massachusetts. He assured me that I would like it there, since the owner hired mostly a Southern staff and the ratio of women to men was four to one. He gave me a name and phone number to call. I did, and talked to a guy named Mario who told me they could use some people on the ground crew. So now it was time to talk my roommate, Rand, and another buddy, J. T. Blanchard, into heading north with me.

Rand and I had done several crazy things during the year, like sneaking into the girls' dorm after hours (nearly getting caught), and almost joining the Marine Corps during the spring break. In the latter instance we had just returned from a baseball trip to the Marine Training Center at Parris Island, S.C. We had been really impressed with the pomp and ceremony there. The crisp steps of the Corps in review and the band playing the Marine Hymn brought goose pimples to even the most skeptical critic of the military. One of our classmates, Glenn Laudermilk, was a veteran and Marine Reserve lieutenant. Glenn had presented us with a terrific proposition. We could join the Marine Reserves, have a paid summer job, and get our basic training over with. Best of all, we could remain in college until we earned our degrees and surely by the time we went on active duty the war in Korea would be over. We didn't learn until much later that Glenn was using us to demonstrate a power-of-persuasion theory as a psychology class project.

At the beginning of spring break we reported to the Marine Reserve unit in Atlanta for physical exams and filling in all the pre-induction forms. Rand was ecstatic: he had been overwhelmed by the graduation ceremony at Parris Island. As Glenn told us, applying his skills of persuasion, a Marine grows a foot taller as he marches past the reviewing stand with the band playing the Marine Hymn.

After the paperwork part of the induction process was completed, all that remained was our physical, being sworn in, and issued uniforms. I didn't especially look forward to getting a uniform; my experience in high school ROTC was a sufficient amount of spit and shine for a lifetime. Rand, though, had attended a small high school in rural Georgia and had never been in a regimented environment. He saw the uniform as a symbol of success and maturity. I had to agree, the uniform had the power to make boys think they were men; and Rand, with his clean cut features and muscular build, could compete with the best of the Marine Corps posters.

The Naval Air Station in Atlanta was where all Navy and Marine recruits from the Atlanta area took physicals. We were driven there by a Marine recruiter and were told to call him when we finished, to return with our reports, and be inducted into the Reserves that night.

The stench of naked bodies stuffed into tight lines like cattle in boxcars was reason enough to make even the most ambitious candidate want to cut and run. To me it was like the hot, muggy days in Savannah that caused sweat to fill every crevice of my body. The stifling heat and tension showing in all of the faces made these young men appear less to be future heroes than young men who still remembered their mother's embrace. Rand was just behind me as they took our height and weight and examined our eyes, mouth, ears, and rear end. Things went well until the time came for drawing blood and checking blood pressure. It wasn't a pleasant feeling having a needle stuck in my arm but I was passed on to the next station. Rand was held up a long time with the doctor taking blood as I moved on. After finally being able to give a urine sample and getting a chest x-ray, I was finished with the exam and told I was fit to be a Marine.

I didn't see Rand again until I went to the dressing area. He was there, already dressed. He had failed the exam because the doctor couldn't get the needle into his arm, and after several attempts he had passed out. All of the excitement and frustration had pushed Rand's blood pressure far above the acceptable level.

Rand was bitterly disappointed that he was not accepted. I tried to convince him that this wasn't a big deal, that he could try again during the summer and probably make it, but my pep talk fell on deaf ears. He urged me to embark on the military life alone; I was a better man than he was, and he was doomed to failure. But my own enthusiasm for Marine Corps pageantry had vanished. I couldn't find the number to call for the ride back to the Marine Reserve unit, but I did find a big trash can as we waited for the bus that would take us to the train station and me back to Savannah for the spring holidays. Into the can went all of the papers we had been issued by the Marines, and we sighed with relief as we realized we had regained our sanity.

Now it's the end of the school year, and I'm trying to convince Rand and J.T. what a great prospect it is to work at a summer resort in New England.

"Let's go, Rand," I implored. "Damn it, let's give it a try." He was the one balking. J.T. seemed willing to go right off the bat.

"I don't know, Claxton, that place can't be as good as he says it is. The pay's not all that great, and I don't believe that crap about four women to every man."

J.T. pondered that for a moment. In his high-pitched voice, which seemed totally out of character for a six-foot, 225-pound catcher, he said: "I'd like to go even if they only have two women for each man. It looks like we're all going to be in the Army next year anyway, so we may as well enjoy this last summer. And nobody else is going to pay much better."

Rand signed. He really didn't need much convincing. "You're right, J.T. That Korea thing just goes on and on. I can't believe it's lasted so long, until you look back on all our friends who've joined the Navy or Air Force. Okay, I'm with you."

That matter settled, our celebration of the day's baseball victory continued.

"You want another beer, J.T.?" I asked.

"Hell, yeah, let's hang one on," J.T. replied. "We don't beat the Citadel cadets every day."

The beer had been slipped into the dormitory after the game past the watchful eyes of Captain Mack, the dormitory proctor. Our last game of the season had been one of our most satisfying, and now the cold beer was adding to the day's pleasure.

"You pitched a great game, Rand, but I thought we were gone when they went ahead in the ninth inning."

Rand agreed. "They were just lucky to get that hit off me, and wouldn't have if you hadn't slipped, Claxton. Normally you'd get that ball."

J.T. laughed. "Yeah, and normally he would strike out rather than get the winning hit."

"I asked Coach to let somebody hit for me. Know what he said? 'I would if I *had* anybody.' Sure made me feel great!"

"Don't get pissed, he was playing percentages. You already had one hit in the game, so the odds were against you getting another one."

The look the coach gave me was, "All is probably lost, but the rules say you've got to go to bat." There were runners on second and third with only one out. The infield was in close to try to get the tying run at the plate. The pitcher didn't seem to be afraid of my power and was throwing hard down the middle. I took a strike, and then took a lusty swing at the next pitch. The sound of my bat meeting the ball wasn't the solid crack that a batter likes to hear, but more of a thud. I hit under the ball and lifted it over the pitcher's head. With the infield charging, the ball got by them and slowly rolled to center field. Rand and J.T. both scored and we had a 4 to 3 win over the Cadets.

"In the annals of Coyee's glorious sports history," said Rand, lifting his beer, "we'll be remembered as immortals."

"If we have to go to Korea we'll probably be remembered as casualties, and I want to have a good time before then."

"You've had too much beer, Claxton. Those stories about all the women at Handover are getting to you."

"One thing's for sure. We'll always need the money, and four to one odds are great if you're horny as I am, so let's have another beer and start packing."

The commencement weekend was the highlight of the school year. One of the featured events was a baseball game between the Coyee varsity and alumni. The old grads who had played baseball loved to recall their moments of glory, and if they had played long enough ago they were sure to have batted above .400. My only question was, if they were so good why had Coyee never won a conference baseball championship?

The annual alumni-varsity game was scheduled on the day we wanted to leave for the resort. If we missed that Saturday bus, we had to wait until Monday for the next one. When we told Coach we wouldn't be able to play in the game, he got very angry and threatened to kick us off the team. For some reason, he would rather beat the alumni than anyone else we played . . . maybe because of the humiliation he had suffered when the alumni upset his varsity team five years before. After a lecture about team responsibility and spirit, he finally accepted the fact that we needed summer jobs to earn money for the next school year, and that the job called for us to be in Massachusetts on Monday. At the end, he even offered to pick us up at 4:00 in the morning and drive us to the bus station.

We were too excited to sleep, and stayed up all night talking and getting packed. Coach arrived on time and seemed a little disappointed to see us ready to go. He still had hopes that we would change our minds and play in the alumni game.

At 4 a.m. the township of Walaholla, South Carolina, with its outdated streetlights and graveyard-like silence, had to be the loneliest place in the world. After we got our bags out of the car, Coach shook hands with us and told us to stay in good condition for next year. "Try not to have too much fun" was his parting bit of advice, as if he knew the consequences of too much pleasure. In the cool and quiet of the morning, as Coach drove away, our last chance to back out was gone and the reality struck home that we were leaving our friends and familiar surrounds and heading north to the unknown.

The bus arrived almost on time, but the driver gave us a bit of bad news. This was not the express bus to New York City; we would be going there via Washington, D.C. That added a half day to the travel time. As the bus made the turn on Highway 29, we passed by the Walaholla Mule Trading Barn. Years ago the owners had painted, on the eaves of the barn, a picture of two mules facing each other. From time to time, students at Coyee would paint huge penises on the mules. The owners would paint over these adaptations, but an image would always manage to show through regardless of the number of cover-up coats. As the bus picked up speed and Walaholla faded in the background, I still saw in my mind the mules with their dongs dragging the ground. I thought maybe we did need to try a new environment.

The bus arrived at New York City at noon on Sunday. We had experienced delay, breakdown, and heavy traffic only to learn that the connecting bus to Pittsfield, Massachusetts, did not leave until 10 o'clock that evening. We then had to decide what to do for the next ten hours. J.T. wanted to see the Yankees play but they were out of town. Several people told us the Dodgers were at home, but we were a little afraid to venture as far as Brooklyn. We had heard some bad things about the Brooklyn subways, and weren't big Dodger fans anyway. Finally, we decided to go to Radio City Music Hall and see a movie and the Rockettes.

Even with a map of Manhattan that we bought at the Port Authority bus terminal, getting to the Radio City Music Hall proved to be more of a problem than any of us expected. We were able to put our luggage in a locker before we left the bus station and planned to walk to save the bus fare. The streets were packed with all types of people. I couldn't believe that so many would be downtown on Sunday, but I soon realized that this is where those people lived.

Our first encounter with a native New Yorker was on the corner as we crossed the street from the bus station. We were offered the buy of a lifetime from this sleazy character with a two-day growth of beard and hair down to his shoulders. He had what he said was a solid gold watch that he would sell us for $50. He said the watch was "hot" and he had to get rid of it right away. We may not have looked like three refugees from the South, but we couldn't have raised $50 for *any* bargain. I had only $5 and I'm sure no one else was better off.

Eventually, despite a few wrong turns, we found ourselves at Broadway and 42nd Street, just a block from Times Square. This spot was familiar to me from the radio broadcasts on New Year's Eve, when the announcer, Ben Grower, would count down the last ten seconds of the old year and welcome in the new.

There was a plaque on the corner of one of the streets joining Times Square that stated that Eugene O'Neill was born and grew up at this location. Rand and J.T. were not impressed with the fact that I knew who he was. I tried to explain that many of his plays had been performed just down the street on Shubert Alley where most of the theaters are. I would like to have seen "South Pacific" which was playing at the Majestic Theater, but even if we had the money the play was sold out.

Our priorities were first to find Rockefeller Center and then a place to eat. The Empire State Building was out after we were told that there was a two hour wait to get to the observation tower.

And then we were at Rockefeller Center, which was even more impressive than I had envisioned. I knew there wouldn't be ice skating in June, but I didn't expect the ice skating area to be converted into an outdoor dining room. There was a short wait for a table as we began to realize that maybe we were at the wrong restaurant. Families having dinner after church, young couples out on the town, and a few groups of elegantly dressed women. Our blue jeans, short-sleeved shirts, and penny loafers were much in contrast to the setting. A waiter with a French accent and dressed in a tuxedo reluctantly seated us in a far corner where we were to be as much out of sight as possible. Our view of the other diners (and vice versa) was blocked by a floral arrangement, but in the other direction we could see the Newsweek and NBC buildings.

Our exit from the restaurant was much quicker and less obvious than our entrance. We were not prepared for the prices on the menu. A roast beef sandwich was $2.50, and there was nothing cheaper. Hungry as we were, we quietly departed. Fearing that we might be charged for the table, we sneaked out one at a time.

Just off Rockefeller Center we found the best buy in New York, a 25-cents hot dog from a street vendor. I'm not sure how many Rand and J.T. ate, but I put away four in about as many minutes. The smell of the grease burning on the charcoal, and of freshly cut onions on hot mustard, combined with the taste of a cold orange soda, made for a feast to be remembered.

We finally reached the Music Hall in time for the matinee show. I had expected a much larger theater but it wasn't much bigger than the Lucas in Savannah and was nothing compared to the Fox in Atlanta.

The movie was based on Theodore Dreiser's book, *An American Tragedy*, and starred a young and beautiful Elizabeth Taylor and Montgomery Clift, who played the role of Clyde very well. I had read the book in high school but appreciated the final scene even more as Elizabeth Taylor visited Clyde on death row. It made one realize how unfair life could be.

I'll have to admit that, exhausted from the all-night trip, I slept through some of the movie, but was awake for the ending and then really jolted awake when the lovely and leggy Rockettes came on stage.

The overnight trip was uneventful except that I saw some of the most beautiful scenery of my life in the Hudson Valley as the moonlight touched the mountains and river near West Point. I was still awake when we reached Albany, N.Y., for another delay and bus change. After three days on the bus, nights and days all ran together, but about daylight the driver woke us up with the announcement that we were in Pittsfield, Massachusetts, just a few miles from the resort where we would work.

Chapter Two

 Welcome to Handover

After a short wait and a badly needed cup of coffee, we were picked up at Pittsfield by a driver from the Handover resort. He introduced himself as Tony, and said he was a student in a Virginia college and a summertime worker at the resort. Without our asking, he immediately began to tell us what we would initially need to know about Handover and the staff.

"There are three guys you want to avoid," he said, as we turned onto a dirt road that led to Handover. "Murphy the chef is mean as hell and gives everybody a hard time. Stanley the headwaiter is two-faced, and will stab you in the back. Mike the ground crew chief is just plain crazy."

"How long have you worked at Handover?" asked J.T.

"This will be my fourth summer. I started while I was in high school, working with the ground crew with Mike, and then went into the kitchen last year with Harry."

"Why haven't you got a waiter's job? I thought they made the most money," said Rand as he began to rouse himself from a deep sleep.

"They do make the best money, but they are all jerks. If you don't kiss Stanley's ass, he can get you run off. I'd rather work in the kitchen where I know what's happening. It's simple there—Murphy hates *everybody*."

"What about the women? We were told there were four women to every man."

"Don't worry, there will be more than you can handle."

"I'd like to see *that* day," said J.T.

"You will. Right now there are just a few guests, but wait two more weeks and we'll be swamped with them."

"Why two more weeks?" asked J.T., in a tired but eager voice.

"People from the city—New York City—just don't take vacations in June when the weather is like this, cold and rainy. They wait until the Fourth of July weekend, which begins about six weeks of good weather."

"Now, if you look off to the right after we make the next curve, you can see the Mansion, which is the main building at Handover. We're already on Handover property, by the way. Mario has been able to buy back all the land of the original 1600-acre estate. That's Mount Greylock behind the Mansion, the highest mountain in Massachusetts."

As one who had seen some beautiful plantations around Charleston, the stately old Atlanta homes, and even the Biltmore House in Asheville, I must say I was certainly impressed by this part of Massachusetts. Not on the scale of the Biltmore, but certainly beyond anything we had been led to expect in rural Massachusetts.

The pointed iron picket fence seemed a mile long as we came to the main entrance. After seeing the iron fence I had expected an ornate entrance with uniformed guards. The entrance turned out to be quite simple, just two brick pillars with sliding gates and a security guardhouse.

However, the driveway to the Mansion, lined with Hawaiian lamps, was as impressive a driveway as I'd ever seen.

The gradual slope of manicured lawn and softball fields led to an unusual structured building with two long wings closing in the courtyard and a split rail fence surrounding it. Tony told us it had been the stables and now was the Tally-Ho Club where there was dancing every night. Behind the Tally-Ho were rows of cottages and a clear mountain lake.

We made a right turn and passed a par-three golf course and a tennis complex before the final drive around the circle to the Mansion. As Tony brought the station wagon to a stop in front of the Mansion, we all felt a moment of satisfaction and relief. We had finally arrived.

After a brief introduction to the office staff, we were led to the staff dining room. The staff had finished breakfast and the kitchen was closed to them. We soon learned about Murphy the chef—he refused to serve us. "Not here on time, you don't eat," was his policy. But thanks to Tony, our driver, we were able to get some cold leftovers and much needed rest. Staff personnel were quartered in old Army surplus tents behind the mansion, and there we met our tent mate Monk. He was still in bed, and mumbled something about having the morning off. The tents were nothing elegant, but for now any place to sleep would do.

The next two weeks were like a forced labor camp. We did every type of maintenance job imaginable. Cutting grass was a daily assignment, as was tending to the tennis courts and swimming pool, but the new guys, meaning us, got the short end of the stick. We painted the Mansion, put tar on its roof, and cleaned its boiler room and drainage system.

It didn't take us long to learn the ropes. If you worked hard and finished a job early, you were rewarded by being given another hard job. So you learned early to get smart—hide someplace, slow down, take it easy, anything to avoid Mike, the ground crew chief.

The best part of the two weeks was meeting the staff. After having a tent party every night, I didn't care if the guests came or not. At first, breakfast at 7:00 was a big deal, being much more sumptuous than at college. Typically, we might have eggs, bacon, pancakes, orange juice, hash brown potatoes, and all we could eat. But the novelty soon wore off, and after two weeks of drinking and staying up late, we stayed in bed until Mike came after us.

Finally, everything was painted, repaired, and ready for the big July 4th weekend. We quickly learned that Saturday mornings were the most hectic time at Handover, with new guests arriving and old ones checking out. Saturday mornings also followed the frustrations of Friday night. Many guests had hangovers, and others were disgusted because they didn't have the good time they expected and had to return to work after a disappointing vacation. Ironically, the most frustrated of all might have been those who had a great vacation, enjoying a romantic encounter during the week. But then reality struck. The romantic couple might live hundreds of miles apart, and even if they lived in the same city, things could not be the same as they had been at the resort. Parents, jobs, and a confined life would not let things happen as they did at the resort . . . this, after all, was Massachusetts in the early 1950's.

Rand was shaking me.

"Claxton, you'd better get up if you want breakfast."

"I don't think I ever want to get up again unless the weather warms up."

"Do you sleep in your clothes every night, even your socks?"

"Damn right, if it keeps me warm. These tents feel like the North Pole."

"They're old Army surplus from World War I, probably the same kind the Army is still using. Come on, get up, it's not that cold."

"I can't believe the weather up here is so lousy in the summer. After two days on that hot bus I was hoping for some cooler weather, but this is ridiculous. The temperature hasn't gone above 60 degrees since we've been here, and it must be freezing this morning."

"You've just got thin blood. You need to eat more of this Yankee food to toughen you up."

"If I have to eat hash brown potatoes and broccoli again, I think I'll throw up. Why can't they fix some decent Southern food?" I was still annoyed about our bus trip. "You know, Rand, the trip up here would have really been interesting if we could have stopped in Washington."

"I'd rather stay over in New York, like we did."

"Not me. I was surprised that the bus went right by the monuments in Washington. I wish we could have stopped at the Lincoln and Washington monuments."

"Maybe you can get stationed there when we go into the Army. I'll still take New York."

"You can have it . . . ten hours was enough of that place for me."

"At least I saw some women there, which is more than I can say for Handover. I told you that guy in Savannah was lying, Claxton."

"You don't seem to be doing too badly with Janet. You're with her every night, and I can't remember the last time you got in before me. You and Monk are the only guys making out while the rest of us suffer."

"Monk may be making out, but all I get is the story of her old boyfriend who is in the Navy, and also that the staff girls can't fool around. I had hopes for J.T. with the nurses, but it looks like he has become their full-time chauffeur."

"Can you believe that Monk? I never see him come in at night, so he must be up to something. He's like everyone I've ever known from South Carolina—crazy as hell. But what else would you expect from a guy who grew up in a town called Ninety-six and spent every summer at Myrtle Beach?"

"Mike says the women will be here this week for sure. The big crowds don't come in June because of the bad weather."

"What difference does it make anyway, Rand? We'd still get the shitty ground crew jobs and miss all the women. Why didn't we try to get waiter jobs so we could have first choice rather than taking what's left over?"

"Ah, stop bitching, Claxton, and get dressed. If Monk can make out as things have been, surely we can score with four-to-one odds."

J.T. had been assigned the job of driving one of the station wagons this morning. It was the first week of July and the big crowds of the summer were finally arriving. Picking up luggage and getting guests to the railroad stations on time was an important part of the Handover operation. With a full house expected, it would be disastrous to have many of them stranded, for there just wasn't any room available. Mario Beanko had learned early, as owner and manager, that it was better business to overbook and have a few angry people without rooms than to lose money on cancelled reservations.

J.T. had waited until 11 o'clock to make his last pickup at the School House Cottage where two nurses from Boston had stayed for three weeks. They must have gotten a special rate to stay for so long, for the crowd had been small early in the season and they didn't seem to have much fun. If they had been attractive, someone on the staff would have made a try to score because there were far more men than women this early in the season. One was a big redhead with freckles; the other was a thin brunette with a large nose and thick eyeglasses. Not really unattractive, but they still could not get much attention.

The nurses didn't have a car, so J.T. had to drive them almost everywhere they went. They found many things to do off the resort, such as attending summer stock theater and dance and music festivals. They were more interested in these activities than the ones at the resort. Since Handover furnished transportation to the festivals, J.T. was on call every night. The consequences were often frustrating. Several times at the Tally-Ho, the old stable that had been turned into a dance hall, he found someone who looked good and seemed willing. He would have to leave to pick up the nurses only to return and find the girl drunk and with someone else.

J.T. had really become hostile toward the nurses. Not only had they ruined several nights for him, but they continually questioned him about life in the South, campus life for men and women; and even teased him about his high-pitched voice. J.T. was a good baseball catcher and had shown big-league potential until he hurt his shoulder and throwing arm. He had signed a contract with the Yankees, but once he hurt his arm the pros lost interest in him. Two things bothered him—his high-pitched voice and his small penis. He had taken a lot of riding about his voice at games, but no one in the locker room ever commented about the size of his penis. At six-feet-four and 225 pounds, he took no crap from wise guys.

As the luggage was being loaded onto the truck that would take it to the railroad station, J.T. slowly drove the station wagon toward the School House Cottage for his last contact with the nurses. He was a better than average looking guy—tall, blond, and muscular—and could live with his high-pitched voice and small penis, but at the age of twenty he was tired of jacking off and desperately needed a woman. His frustration was compounded by the fear that he might not satisfy her. Most guys masturbated with their full hand, but he used only his thumb and two fingers. He had been at the resort three weeks without even getting close to a woman, despite all the talk that there was more pussy here than you could handle.

It was only 11 o'clock, so he wasn't as rushed as he thought he would be. Perhaps he had overlooked an opportunity with the nurses, since they had tried to be friendly on the way back to the dance festival. When they had asked him in for a drink, he declined the offer so that he could rush back to a live prospect at the Tally-Ho—only to find her with someone else. But today if he took the nurses directly to the railroad station, he wouldn't be missed until after lunch, and this would give him two hours with them. After all they had been friendly, and he realized he had been dumb not to take advantage of the situation.

The School House Cottage was off the main road. It had once been a small private school for staff children when Handover was a private estate. It had only two large guest rooms, and one side had been empty while the nurses where there. He had driven the nurses to the cottage when they arrived three weeks earlier. He knew that the heavy solid door to the cottage opened to a foyer and the inner glass door opened to the bedroom. New England houses were usually built this way, to keep the winter cold from rushing into the house when someone entered.

J.T. opened the heavy door without knocking and found the luggage stacked in the foyer. He had hoped to get a quick look at the nurses dressing, and wasn't disappointed. Through the curtain on the glass door he could clearly see both girls completely naked sitting on the bed. The red-haired girl had untied her hair, and it almost covered her broad shoulders. She was big boned and had enormous breasts with huge nipples. The dark-haired girl was toward the headboard of the bed. Without her glasses and clothes she looked great. Her shoulders were thin, with small firm breasts that almost turned up.

Their giggles and laughter indicated they had been drinking rather heavily. Three glasses sat on the table; and between the girls, also naked, lay Red Kelly, a 45 year-old beer salesman from Boston. Red had been to Handover every weekend for the last five years. He really rubbed it in later that the nurses had been there three weeks and the young studs couldn't score, but it took a 45 year-old to satisfy them.

J.T. moved over closer to the door, for the threesome was too involved to see him. He watched for what seemed like an awful long time. His heart was pounding and he got the sensation that all his blood was rushing into his penis.

As the threesome reached a howling climax and fell to the bed exhausted, J.T. suddenly found a huge penis in his hand that caused his knees to buckle when it erupted.

The luggage would never be the same.

Chapter Three

 Girls and Showers

It was a cool afternoon. The sun was bright but the temperature barely reached 80 degrees, which meant that everybody by the pool had to keep moving to keep comfortable. A four-piece musical group, the Stumpers, had been playing since 1 o'clock and was really getting warmed up as it swung into "Mack the Knife" and "Hello dolly," favorites of a new guest who had just checked in.

The pool was the best place to meet new people and make friends at the resort. The ratio of females to males was indeed high—the guest list was 80 percent women, so the girls who were looking for male companionship tried to get acquainted as soon as possible. A nearby volleyball game gave the guys a chance to show off whatever athletic skills they possessed and get a view of all the new arrivals. So the game began on a beautiful Saturday afternoon—men and women, mostly from large cities, with a week ahead of them to party together, to eat together, to play all kinds of sports together, and hopefully to sleep together.

"Attention, please. Good afternoon, everyone. Welcome to Handover. I'm Don Williams, your social director," came a genuine Southern drawl over the public address system. "My staff and I have lined up a very active week for you to help make your vacation at Handover an experience you'll remember."

"At 3 o'clock today on the North Forty pasture behind the Tally-Ho, Major John O'Hara of the U. S. Air Force will fly an F-80 jet fighter in a demonstration of strafing and attack bombing. Major O'Hara, who was a guest at Handover last week, is a Korean War ace who shot down nine MIGs. Our staff is lining off the target area now, and the show will begin sharply at 3 o'clock.

"At 4 o'clock we will have the first softball game of the week between the staff team and the guest all-stars. At 5 o'clock, happy hour begins in the Carriage Room in the mansion, where everyone meets and gets acquainted before dinner. Our traditional Saturday night barbecue will be served at 6 o'clock in the pine grove. Bob Murphy, our chef, has gone all out tonight for a great dinner—lobster, steaks, and all the trimmings you like in a barbecue.

At 9:00 until 1:00 in the Tally-Ho, there will be dancing and merry-making with Rex Robinson and his band. From 1:00 'til 3:00 in the morning, wind down in the Carriage room with the Stumpers; and if you're hungry, have breakfast at one of the late restaurants in town."

Handover had been the summer home of a New York banker back when wealthier New Yorkers had homes in Newport and Florida as well as the Berkshires. As his family died out, the handsome mansion with its 1600 acres of New England countryside was sold several times—initially to a private school and eventually to Mario Beanko, who converted it into a summer resort.

Aside from the anticipated need for extensive painting and repair, two major obstacles confronted the satisfactory operation of the resort: the water supply and sewage treatment system. Mario was able to convince the city fathers that the taxes from the resort would justify water service from Pittsfield, but they were not interested in adding a commercial venture to an already overworked sewage treatment plant. The standard-sized septic tank at Handover had been satisfactory for a summer home and adequate for a private school, but was woefully inadequately for a summer resort. The addition of new bathrooms in the mansion, and the building of ten new cottages and other structures, had so overloaded the system that the drainage field was like an open sewer.

Rand and I had worked in the drain field all morning putting out lime and other chemicals to kill the bacteria and trying to cut back the roots and weeds that hindered drainage. Being the newest arrivals, we had been literally given the shittiest job at the resort by Mike, who was also in charge of maintenance. At times today, we had been knee-deep in solid waste.

"Are you and Becky going to the movie tonight, Claxton?"

"No, she turned me down. Told me that all four of the Virginia girls have plans with the waiters at the big party in Tent One."

"You mean the Virginia Virgins stay together as a group?"

"Yes, but who cares about them now? Monk told me that women have been coming in all morning and that the pool is covered with them."

"Yeah, I'll bet he said they were all good looking, too."

"What else would you expect Monk to say?"

"I hope Mike doesn't have another job for us like this morning. I'm not going back to that damn drainage field again. Let's take the truck and lawn mowers down behind the Pump House cottage and hide for the rest of the afternoon. Mike will be taking guests and luggage to their rooms and won't be thinking about us."

"That sounds good, but for now let's go back to the tent and grab a little nap before our lunch hour is over, just in case we don't get to sleep this afternoon. I'm worn out!"

Mario Beanko had come to the United States from the Lake Como region of northern Italy in 1910. At an early age he had worked as a stable hand for his father, a horse trainer. He continued in that job after his father emigrated with his family to America and became a horse trainer for a circus. Mario quickly became an expert rider and an excellent showman. He often demonstrated both characteristics for his guests in rides on his beautiful white stallion.

Major O'Hara had arrived at Handover driving a white Packard convertible and wearing full-dress uniform with all battle awards displayed. Mario, the showman, immediately saw the advertising potential of this war hero and offered him free accommodations for a week. The major took full advantage of the attention given him at every happy hour, dinner, and dance. He drove his gleaming Packard convertible everywhere, even the 200 yards from the Mansion to the Tally-Ho where Mario introduced him every night.

When Major O'Hara left on Saturday morning, Mario had pictures taken of himself and staff surrounding the major and the white convertible. To show his appreciation of Mario's hospitality, Major O'Hara offered to demonstrate his flying skills in a mock bombing and strafing attack over the north pasture of the resort. He left a drawing showing how the target area should be marked off.

Mario was beside himself with excitement. What could better impress the first big crowd of the season? Maybe the local press would cover it. But first he had to get Mike and his crew to get the north pasture ready by 3 o'clock. Things had to be just right for the major; he flew with precision and exactness, as was clearly indicated in the diagramed plan he gave Mario.

"Claxton, Rand, get out of those bunks and get ready to go back to work."

"It's not time yet, Mike."

"Hell it isn't—it's ten minutes past one. You should have met me at the tool shed like you did this morning."

"I'm not going to work in that drainage field any more today. That's all the stink I can take in one day."

"Forget that, we've got something more important to do this afternoon. Mario wants the pasture below the Tally-Ho lined off with marble dust for the air show. J.T. and Monk are going to help us, but it's got to be finished by 3 o'clock."

"What about the luggage we were supposed to pick up at the railroad station?"

"It will just have to wait. I got the marble dust in town during lunch, and we're ready to go. Mario wants this done now, so you guys get ready and let's get on it."

When we arrived at the pasture, we found that the riding horses had been moved there only that morning for grazing. This upset Mike considerably.

"Oh Jesus, who the hell put those damn horses down here?"

"Not us, we worked in the sewer all morning. How about you, J.T.?"

"I was driving guests around all morning."

"That's a lot of bull," said Monk. I was driving too, and all I saw was your station wagon parked at the School House Lodge where those nurses were staying.

"Did you make out with both of them, J.T.?" asked Rand.

"He didn't do *anything*," Monk said. Red Kelly bragged to everybody at lunch that he banged both nurses this morning."

"Alright you guys, knock it off. J.T., you take the truck, drive down the hill, and open the gate that goes back to the barn. We'll form a wide half-circle and try to run them to the gate. You cover the sides with the truck if any of the horses get outside our line."

J.T., who usually kept control of his temper, was furious at Monk's remarks about his failure with the nurses. He took out his frustration by driving the truck with no regard whatever for safety, reason, and sanity.

"Mike, how are four of us going to get ten horses to that gate?"

"Just spread out, yell at them, wave your arms, that sort of shit—they'll run down the hill."

Monk demonstrated his lack of athletic ability as he joined Mike with all the vigor of youth. His short legs, pumping like the pistons of a toy train, and chubby body were no match for the agile and crafty horses. But what he lacked in physical ability was far exceeded by his courage, or more aptly foolishness, as he ran among the horses with reckless abandon. Several times he was almost trampled by the skittery stallions. As dangerous as his efforts were, the presence of comic relief in deciding whether Monk was chasing the horses or vice versa dispelled our fears and proved Monk's lunacy.

"Horses are stubborn and smart," puffed Rand. "They're not going back to the barn until feeding time."

"Damn it, stop talking and get after them!" Mike shouted.

"Oh hell, I stepped in a pile of horse shit."

"That shouldn't bother you, Rand, after working in it all morning."

"Keep moving, don't let them get outside of us," yelled Mike, as he gave a good impression of a rodeo clown, arms flapping, jumping like a child on a trampoline, and running around like a headless chicken.

"Look out, here comes J.T. driving like a wild man. Hey, J.T., it's me—Claxton! Don't hit me! Doesn't Mike know that those damn horses don't want to go back to the barn?"

"I wouldn't either if someone was there waiting to ride me," said Rand.

The roundup eventually ended after a great deal of our cussing the horses and whacking them with anything available. Those ten horses wound up nearly exhausting us five men.

We were running out of time as well as energy, so we lined off the flight path by dumping the marble dust from the moving truck. By the time we finished, both the truck and its inhabitants were covered with a coat of white dust. At 2:45, a quarter of an hour before show time, we finished the last safety marker. The crowd was beginning to gather on a grassy bank that overlooked the pasture. To them we must have looked like gray-haired ghosts.

From our vantage point, a range of hills called Jacob's Ladder led outward to Mount Greylock, one of the most beautiful sights in Massachusetts. Don Williams was on the scene with a bullhorn, giving a detailed description of what was to happen. Major O'Hara was to come from the northeast, directly from Mount Greylock, at an altitude of 500 feet. He would drop down to almost ground level as he approached and release sacks of flour onto the marked targets. He would pull his F-80 jet into a steep climb as he approached the tree-lined bank where the crowd sat, turn sharply, and make another approach to the target area from the southwest.

By 3:30, eyes were getting a little strained from searching the northeast skies for the major's plane, and ears were getting tired of hearing Don Williams' repeated description of what we were about to see. Most everyone had brought extra drinks, but by 3:45 these were gone and the crowd was rapidly losing interest in the air show. Why waste an afternoon in a field when you could be at the pool? Don Williams finally announced that the air show was cancelled because of technical difficulties with the major's plane.

Mario closed the door to his office, with only his wife as company. He had opened a bottle of Chevis Regal scotch to celebrate the major's flight, but the celebration was cancelled after a distressing phone call. The great promotion would have to wait another day, because the state police had arrested a man posing as Major John O'Hara. The suspect had stolen the car and clothing two weeks earlier in Boston and was caught while registering at the Red Lion Inn at Stockbridge, about seven miles away.

"I didn't mind the guy being a liar or thief by taking the free week, but I hope the son of a bitch gets ten years for fucking me today," growled Mario as he finished his fifth scotch.

"Do you think we'll ever get this truck clean?"

"I don't care about the truck, I just hope I can get this dust out of my hair."

"Give me a hand, Claxton, on this big lawn mower. Let's load it up and get out of here before Mike finds us."

"After that screwed-up air show I don't think Mike cares right now where we are. Have you heard why it was cancelled?"

"Only that there were technical problems with the plane, but I'll bet you that Major O'Hara is a phony. I've always believed that anybody who struts and shows off the way he did is hiding something."

"Who cares, all I want to do is hide until we get off work, eat, and take a nap. If there are as many women here as Monk said there is, I want to be well rested for a big night."

As we unloaded the lawn mowers and parked the truck behind the cottage, two girls who were staying there drove up in their car. It was a 1939 blue Mercury convertible that looked great. We were so carried away with the car that we almost overlooked the girls. They had been at the pool all afternoon and had finished all they had to drink while waiting for the air show.

The shorter girl was Ann Chapell, who had just finished Elmira College and planned to teach special education in White Plains, New York. Ann had a baby face and nice figure, a combination that turned me on. Frances was almost a beautiful blonde, but her cut-off chin and straight hair took too much away from a very nice body.

She had finished her first year of teaching fifth grade in Worcester. Massachusetts.

Both girls were determined to have a good time at Handover. but were somewhat disappointed in what they had seen in the way of men since their arrival that morning. At the pool they had become frightfully aware of the male shortage. Most of the few men available were too old, too fat. or too drunk to get their interest.   Under the circumstances. Rand and I. as dirty as we were. must have looked several cuts above what they had seen. We just might be the two males who could make their vacation a success. For two guys looking for a place to hide from work. an invitation for a drink in their room would be a godsend.

"Where did you get that great looking car?"

"My father bought it for me, and we've been restoring it all year."

"It looks fabulous. If you ever want to sell it, let me know."

"He'd kill me if I sold it. He's put a lot of time into restoring it."

"Well, anyway, I'm Claxton and this is Rand. We're supposed to be working, but we came over this way to hide until quitting time."

"After that fouled up air show, I would think everyone connected with it would be in hiding. I'm Frances and this is Ann."

"We didn't have anything to do with the actual show. but we did line off the field."

"You're the guys who were chasing those poor horses and then stirring up the dust storm. Everybody was laughing at you."

"That's us. I don't think I'll ever get that dust out of my hair. But maybe we could get it out of our throats if you invited us in for a beer."

"We don't have any beer, but come on in. We'll find something cool and wet."

This was the first time I had been in one of the Handover guest cottages, and I was impressed. They had rich red carpeting and their walls were paneled with natural wood.

"This room is very nice. I had no idea these cottages were so large."

"We were lucky to get it. They usually put four people in this size room. What do you like to drink other than beer?"

"We're not big drinkers, but bourbon would be find."

"I've heard that before from Southern men. You're all the same, like: I don't drink much but give me two fingers of bourbon in a washtub."

"How did you know we're from the South?"

"Your accent, of course. Besides, everybody I've met so far on the staff is Southern. You would think we were in Georgia or Mississippi. They even have the Confederate flag flying at the Mansion."

"Well, as to drinking, Rand and I play basketball and baseball at school, and I can tell you that hard training and hard drinking don't mix."

"But you *are* from the South?"

"Rock-solid Dixie."

"Well, let's drink to that."

Ginger ale with a dash of bourbon was like a soft drink, so they added a little soda and called it a "Presbyterian." For a day that had been so far nothing but hard work and confusion, it was turning into the most exciting day of the season. The first round of drinks disappeared quickly, so Ann decided to make the next drinks a little stronger. After all, Southern men were supposed to be great bourbon drinkers, in spite of our protestations of athletic abstinence. I decided we might as well live up to their expectations.

Ann and Frances had attended an all-girls school, and their second-hand impression of male college athletes was that they were muscular dummies. To learn that I was majoring in English and Rand in biology impressed them greatly, and I figured that we were at least to second base with these girls.

"Does anything exciting ever happen at your school, Rand?"

"Freshen up my drink and I'll think of something."

"That's the third round. Do you think that you can handle it? Remember what you said about hard training and drinking."

"We've suspended training for today."

"Come on. What kind of wild things happened on campus?"

"Claxton and I didn't get in on the excitement. We had to be in our rooms early every night."

"I don't believe that. I've heard that baseball players are the wildest athletes of all."

"Maybe at some places, but not at Coyee College."

"Didn't the team ever do anything exciting when you went on road trips to other schools?"

"We did get in on a party after a game in Charleston, but we had to get back to our room before the real fun started."

"Back to your room—you mean a curfew?"

"That's right, especially after we lost a game."

"Did you ever find out what the real fun was?"

"Oh yeah, two guys stayed and got in on it, but were suspended from the team."

"Well, what was it?"

"You really want to know?"

"Sure we do!"

"They had a girl in one of the back rooms who was taking on everybody. These guys waited until five other guys had been with her, and then backed out because she was so ugly."

"Ann, do you believe they backed out?"

"No, and I believe that these are the guys who stayed."

"Not us, but now it's your turn—what's it like at an all-girls' school?"

"Very dull, except behind the gym where everybody went to park with their boyfriends. But the cops made things a little difficult. They seemed to know the best times to drive through and shine their spotlight into the cars."

Rand pondered that for a moment, then gave a big grin.

"Claxton has a good story, if he'll tell it. You know, Clax, the shower story."

"Darn you, Rand," I groaned, "not that one, they'll think we're weird."

"Come on, tell us! Don't be so modest!"

"It's about peeking at girls in a shower," I said, not sure of what their reaction would be.

"Sounds terrific! Let's hear the story!"

"I'll need a strong drink for this."

"No problem except for the ice."

I took a big swallow of my drink and launched into my story.

"Since Coyee College is a church-related school, there are some pretty firm rules regarding campus behavior. Dinner is served at 6 o'clock, and the hours from 7:30 to 9:30 are designated for study. During that time the female students had to be in the dormitory or signed out to the library. From 9:30 until 10:00, the girls had a limited amount of liberty. They could go to the snack bar or coffee shop, or be with friends on the campus grounds. Promptly at 10 o'clock, the house mother rang a hand bell and all the girls were herded in. They usually ran from behind the hedges in warm weather and from cars and vacant classrooms in the winter, trying not to be too obvious about adjusting their clothes."

The 30 minutes was never time enough to make out; it produced a lot of frustration but certainly kept down the number of pregnancies. The founding church fathers seemed to know how to keep the students interested in each other, though—the marriage rate for Coyee graduates is unusually high."

I paused, and the girls looked at each other.

"Interesting story, but where does the weird part come in?"

"I'm getting to that now," I said. "During the spring quarter, someone noted that the window in the girls' shower had been lowered from the top to let out the steam and heat. He also noted that there was a vacant three-storied classroom building directly opposite where the shower room was."

"Oh oh," smiled Frances.

"At first only a few guys knew about the view from room 315, but as word got around, the crowd began to get out of control. As the last girl entered the dormitory, the rush to 315 would begin, but most of the crowd would find all available viewing spaces taken. Finally, someone came up with a system of drawing lots to determine who would watch each night. The rules were simple—no one could watch two nights straight, and no one was to tell anyone else about our peeking. It turned out to be a poorly kept secret, because more guys showed up every night.

"When I finally drew a winning number to get in, I was put in the third row and could hardly see over the other guys' heads. The guy in front of me was Marvin Cain, who was dating one of the German twins who were exchange students at the school.

"With all the steam in the shower room, about the only good view was when the girls entered and left the shower area. There were several showers but no partition, and the angle of view from room 315 made it possible to see only from the shoulders down; therefore a great guessing game developed.

"No sooner had the twelve viewers been selected and taken choirboy positions around the window than the first girl entered the shower. When she stopped at the door to remove her robe, there was complete silence and anticipation among the viewers until we realized it was Big Mary Suttles. She was easy to identify from the shoulders down. Her backside was in full view as she faced the water from the shower head. It was like the rear end of one of those Japanese sumo wrestlers. And when she turned around, we saw two huge breasts that hung almost to her waist.

"The second girl entered as Mary soaped up. Our hopes rose . . . this one had to be better than Big Mary. After a few moments of silence, a disgusted "Oh, shit!"

came from the back row of viewers. The new girl was Betty Rollins, the campus nympho. She had the body of a weightlifter and absolutely no sex appeal, but there were a lot of guys on campus who had decided that she was better than nothing.

"Finally our patience was rewarded. Two girls entered the shower room, and these had slender legs and nice all-over tans. All over except for a couple of thin patches left by their two-piece swim suits, which excited us more than if their bodies had been completely brown. From the shoulders down, these girls looked identical, and it occurred to me, and I'm sure a lot of other people at the same time, that they had to be the German twins. Marvin Cain, the guy in front of me, gasped. Which one of them was he dating, I wondered.

"'Hey, Cain, there's certainly some small tits on those girls!'"

"'Screw you!', he said."

"Mary Suttles and Beth Rollins had finished showering and were drying off. The twins continued to shower and soaped each other's backs as they audibly jabberer in German.

"'Hey Cain, those girls ever scrub your back like that?'"

"'One more smartass remark out of you, Richards, and I'll stomp the shit out of you!'"

"Tom Richards was an Army veteran and older than most of the other guys at school, but still acted like a smart kid just out of basic training. The twins had begun to rinse the soap from their bodies and turned their backs to the water with all the movement needed to remove the soap. This gave onlookers a full frontal view. And they didn't let up on Marvin Cain."

"'Hey, Cain, did you ever make both of them together?'"

"At this point, Cain *exploded*. He lunged for Richards and knocked one of the front-row guys into the window, shattering the glass and sending it everywhere. That, and the noise of the fight, carried over to the girls' dormitory. Trying to separate the fighters only caused more confusion and noise as furniture was shoved around the room. In a matter of seconds every window of the dormitory was filled with girls trying to see the cause of the disturbance.

"Either by accident or through stupidity, someone turned on the lights. This startled the hell out of everyone there, and stopped the fight immediately. The rush to the door was frantic—to be seen and identified meant sure expulsion from school. The girls in the shower figured out what was going on the moment the lights came on in the empty building. They ran screaming from the shower, robes half on, directly to the house mother, who called campus security. From that night on the girls' shower room was closed tight and the old classroom building checked each night by security. And thus ended the great shower escapade."

The girls loved the story. Unfortunately for our party, the ice and ginger ale were gone and the bourbon was running low. Ann poured the last drinks and mixed them then only with water. She tried to sing a college song, which I figured was probably "Mimi the Widow." Her voice was pretty slurred by now. The girls were still in their wet bathing suits and were getting a little chilled as the sun began going down. Until now the drinks and conversation had taken their minds off the chill, but rational conversation was becoming impossible as the booze took full effect. All of us were becoming numb and giggly, and feeling a little wild. Ann and I were sitting on the bed, while Rand and Frances snuggled on the small couch.

"Frances," said Ann in a thick drawl, "do you really believe that these two Southern gentlemen would peek into the girls' shower?"

"Hell no, I believe that's a lot of bull. I don't think these two fine gentlemen would even peek in on two *Northern* girls, much less refined Southern ladies."

I had drunk more than at any other time in my life, but what they were suggesting filtered through to me.

"Hey, give us a chance to prove how really degenerate we are!"

They had had enough to drink to make them daring or foolish and still know what they were doing. They wanted to tease us a little without letting the situation get out of control.

"Why not," said Frances as she finished her drink. "We'll give you a show to remember, won't we Ann?"

Ann wasn't as enthusiastic as Frances, but what was there to lose? This was her first real vacation since school, and she was determined to have a good time.

"Our show has rules," said Frances as she staggered toward the bathroom. "You are only to *look* unless invited to touch, and you are to stay out of the bathroom until the door is opened . . . then you can walk up to the door and look in. Okay?"

At this point, Rand and I would have agreed to anything to get a show like this started. But whether we'd stick to the rules remained to be seen—aside from anything else, we needed a shower too. Ann, a bit bolder now that there were rules, entered the shower room with a provocative roll of the hips.

Their cottage had a huge bathroom, furnished with fancy old hotel-type plumbing.   The shower, with its adjustable head for pulsation, was the only modern fixture. The shower area, large enough to hold four people, was enclosed with fogged glass through which we saw distorted but tantalizing glimpses of their nude bodies.

After what seemed like an eternity, Frances shouted: "Okay you guys, open the door!" We hastened to do so. What we saw cleared a little of the alcoholic fog from my brain. The view of the German twins from room 215 had been good, but this was terrific. They were soaping each other with all sorts of suggestive moves. Ann would soap her large breasts and push them up to wash her neck. Frances dropped the soap purposely and leaned over to pick it up with her rear facing us. Rand and I had been a little drowsy, but this show completely wakened us.   After Frances dropped the soap the third time, we could no longer restrain ourselves. Off came our clothes, but the shower door was suddenly slammed shut and locked from the inside.

"No, no," shouted Frances, "you promised you would stay outside until you were asked in."

"But we're dirty," protested Rand. "We've worked all day and need a shower!"

"Well, go to your own shower!"

"But we want to shower with you. Please open the door!"

The girls were a little afraid, but this was their vacation, and they had paid a pretty good chunk of money to come to the resort and have fun. And anyway, we were wobbly with booze and perhaps not too much of a threat . . .

"Say please once more!"

"Please, please, please, please open the door!"

"We can't open the door because you broke your promise," Frances said.

"Then I'll come in this way," said Rand, pulling over a vanity stool to climb over the partition. The girls started yelling and laughing, and we were en route over the top to the shower when a most unwelcome sound broke through the din. Someone was pounding on the door.

Simultaneously, I mumbled "Oh shit" and Frances yelled, "WHO IS IT?"

"I'm Mike Laotians, the ground crew boss. There's a truck parked out here, and I'm looking for the guys who were driving it."

"Well, we haven't seen them, but if we do we'll let them know you're looking for them."

His voice sounded a bit skeptical as he said, "Well, if you do see them, tell them to get the truck back to the shop right away because the waiters need it to move the food out to the pine grove for the barbecue tonight."

I couldn't hear all the conversation, but I recognized the voice. Mike had ruined our fun, screwed us again.

"Who has the time?" asked Rand from the bed. He had jumped down from the vanity stool and now lay next to Frances, who had run to the bed and rolled up in the sheet for protection and warmth. To our surprise, it was already a quarter to six.

"Goddam it, they start serving dinner in 15 minutes, and they have to move all that food to the pine grove. Those waiters will be after our asses!"

"Then get that truck back fast," said Ann. "Frances and I will see you at the Tally-Ho tonight for the dance."

The dirt road that led back to the Mansion was filled with holes and gullies caused by recent rains. Rand was normally a good driver, having learned on a log skidder when he worked with his dad cutting pulpwood. On this afternoon his driving skills were forgotten as he hit every hole and gully in the road. The lawn mowers almost bounced out of the truck. I had agreed to let him drive because he said he was sober, but this ride had shocked me into sobriety.

The Mansion was surrounded by a 6-foot steel picket fence, and had a big brick entrance with double gates. On Saturdays one gate was kept closed so that every car passing through could be checked, with any non-paying visitors turned away. It was toward that gate that Rand now sped at 60 miles per hour. My concern turned to terror as we bore down on the gate. Rand seemed hellbent on wrecking the truck, for he didn't slow down even when we reached the gate. We slid through the gate on the left two wheels as Rand jammed on the brakes and cut sharply to the left. The man checking cars was covered with dust and left in a state of shock as our truck shot by.

The maintenance shop area and the back of the kitchen were joined by a small graveled parking lot. This area was always busy with deliveries and shop repairs. It was also the loading area for food to be taken to the barbecue in the pine grove. Tonight it was very active, for without the truck the waiters had to carry all the food to the pine grove.

Bob Murphy had been the chef at Handover for five years. He had worked all over the country in better hotels and restaurants, and had come to Handover for his last job before retiring. Earlier in life, he had served in the Navy, where he learned both about food preparation and the use of strong language. If anyone could cuss like a sailor, it was Murphy. Over the years he had grown to hate waiters, and at Handover he had used the full range of his vocabulary, especially on the inexperienced ones. With only 30 minutes left before serving time, Murphy made them start carrying the food to the serving area. He seemed to derive a sadistic pleasure from their vigorous complaints.

Rand and I made our grand entrance with the truck just as they finished carrying the last of the hot foods. Up charged Max, the assistant headwaiter, who had played football at North Carolina State.

"Where in the hell have you funk-offs been with the truck?" he bellowed as he yanked the door open and reached in to pull me out of the cab. I had been in a number of street fights and had expected a hard time from the waiters, but I was hoping that Max wasn't as mean as he looked. A couple of his buddies joined in with "kick their ass" talk as they surrounded the truck.

I certainly didn't like the situation, but instinct told me I had damn better get in the first lick. As Max reached inside the truck, I quickly pulled the door closed again, trapping his hand, then immediately pushed the door open as hard as I could. Max had taken many clouts to the head in his football days, but wasn't prepared for the force of the metal door. He staggered backward and sprawled on the ground. My street-fighter tactic had worked. One good lick and all the fight was gone from Max, as well as his awestruck buddies.

Murphy had been an unnoticed observer and had enjoyed every move I made. As quickly as the fight had started, it had ended, with Murphy stomping out of the kitchen and giving the waiters hell.

"Max, get your as off the ground and load the truck with ice and drinks. You damn waiters get sorrier every year. I don't see how we can make it through the summer. Goddam it, how can I ever serve a meal with these sorry bastards?"

We staggered to our tent and fell into our bunks—dirty, sleepy, and frustrated, but pleased that we had won the first round with the waiters.

Monk and J.T. drove the rest of the day, meeting late trains at Pittsfield and Lenox and getting other late-arriving guests to their rooms. They made the last run at 7:45 and were ready for dinner. The barbecue had gone very well for a crowd that packed the pine grove and needed food badly after drinking all day. The happy hour bunch was late as usual, but all had been served by 8 o'clock, when the staff was fed.

The pay at Handover was modest but the food was excellent. Mario knew from experience that if the staff was unhappy, the feeling would soon be transferred to the guests. His philosophy was to let the staff eat all they wanted, drink in moderation, and enjoy full guest privileges, after which you could very reasonably expect their best effort.

Monk and J.T. were the last staffers to be served. Murphy was on the serving line to be sure that everyone had a good steak. The waiters, especially Stanley, the headwaiter, would run the staff through the serving line any way possible so they could finish and clean up. Murphy asked them about Rand and me and if we were going to make it to the barbecue. If not, he would save us a plate in the kitchen. After our first bad experience with him, when he refused to serve us when we first arrived at Handover, Murphy turned out to be a damn nice guy. When I think back on my summer at the resort, Murphy is one of the better memories. The old bastard really did have a heart.

Chapter Four

 Me vs. the Waiters

The Saturday night party in Tent One had become a tradition over the years. Only key staff members and selected guests were asked to this exclusive bash. Some of the regulars had arrived around 8:30 and set up the bar. Red Kelly, the beer salesman from Boston, always furnished the booze, and for this generosity he had a standing invitation. Tent One parties specialized in exotic drinks with colorful names, such as "Betwixt the Sheets," "Coming Through the Rye," and "Whoof Harted."

All Tent One members were waiters. Stanley and Max were the elders, with Stu McHailly and Brad Lackland entering their third year. The usual procedure was for early arrivals to set up the bar, and the waiters would get in as soon as the dining room and kitchen duties were completed.

Guests at the party would arrive around 9 o'clock. For a little while the setting could be uncomfortable for the new guests because the waiters were still in their uniforms. This was the way the game was planned—to be with the waiters informally on a friendly basis and later feel more inclined toward larger tips. It was a masterpiece of salesmanship and generated a good time for all. After a couple of rounds of the colorfully named drinks, everyone would be comfortable, totally relaxed, and on a first-name basis.

Over the years, Tent One became not only the best furnished tent at Handover, but also better furnished than any guest room. Stanley was in his ninth year and had scavenged every item available. He had managed to get the Chippendale sofa, chairs, and table from the Mansion living room when it was refurnished, and had stolen the bar from the Carriage Room when it was enlarged. Stanley went to veterinarian school for seven years at the University of Florida. He wanted to practice in New York but couldn't pass the state veterinarian exam, so he now spent half of each year at the resort and the other half (the off season) as an intern in a nearby animal hospital.

"Those bastards on the ground crew really fucked us today," said Stanley as he and Max entered the tent. Red had a drink ready for them, which they certainly needed after all the work the missing truck had caused.

"It won't happen again or I'll have Mario straighten those sons-of-bitches out for good or send them home."

Max didn't comment. The less said about the truck the better. His head throbbed with just the thought of the truck.

The crowd arrived quickly after 9 o'clock and the drinks began to flow. Brad and Stu were late since they had to dry silverware after the meal was finished. Brad was a Boston Irishman and had already started drinking Irish whiskey with Murphy. They were serious drinkers and avoided any physical activity (except women) that might interfere with the pleasure of drinking.

Brad, Red, and the Boston crew were crowing about the Red Sox wins yesterday and today over the New York Yankees, the traditional powerhouse of the American

League. Today's victory moved them two games behind the first-place Yankees.

"This is the year," said Brad as he held up his glass in salute to the Red Sox. "With Ted Williams healthy and the best infield in the league, we'll take the pennant this time."

"Bullshit," said Stu. "With Boston's pitching, no infield can stop all the balls hit through it. With all their power, the Yankees will lead the league in home runs and win by ten games."

Al, one of the older waiters, had slipped off work early to get dressed for the party. He was usually the last to arrive, but tonight the surprise was not his early arrival but the beauty of the girl with him. Most of the female guests were average looking, in their mid-twenties, and on the lookout for husbands. Those girls from New York City could easily be spotted, for they were always dressed in the latest fashion and were the best dancers.

Al had spotted her at lunch shortly after she arrived and had spent the afternoon drinking with her by the pool. He had tried to get her to his tent, but time ran out and she was reluctant to start anything since she was about half Al's age. (Al's standing joke was that, being 42, he was able to easily handle *two* 21 year-old girls.)

Red was mixing drinks as fast as possible, but the demand exceeded his ability. His wife Irene had helped him earlier, but she was drinking more than anyone else and was now beyond talking intelligently. She had found out from the housekeeper about Red and his encounter with the nurses, and was disgusted with him. He couldn't get it up for her last night, but screwed two nurses this morning. Before the night was over, Irene vowed, she would show him a thing or two.

Stanley brooded quietly as he drank. He was still pissed off at the ground crew and the extra work he had to do without the truck. He came to life, though, with the arrival of the two older lady guests he had invited. Old Syrup-Mouth, as he was called behind his back, greeted the ladies with all the Southern charm he possessed.

"My goodness, you look so elegant tonight," he drawled, leaning over both of them.

"Oh Stanley, you're so sweet. I just don't know how we would ever do without you. I'm going to tell Mario that if you ever leave, we will cancel our reservations forever."

"Now, now, nobody's irreplaceable," he said, attempting a modest blush.

"I know that, but I would never enjoy another meal here without you serving it. You do so many nice little things for us."

Stanley's smile, his speech, and his suave manner were strictly business. He couldn't be sweet enough to the guests in the dining room, but when they left him an insufficient tip, Old Syrup-Mouth became Old Bad-Mouth.

Brad recalled how at lunch one of the ladies had complained that there was a fly in her ice tea. Stanley, sweet as sugar in the dining room, rushed to the kitchen with the tea glass, plucked the fly out with his fingers, and returned the same glass with a beaming smile. But the time doing even that had caused him to lose a newly arriving group of good tipping customers. "Those damn bitches cost me four times what they're worth," he grumbled.

Both ladies were in their forties and dressed quite nattily for a tent party. They seemed out of place in this noisy and rather youthful environment. In deference to their dignity, the drink urged upon them was "Coming Through the Rye" rather than "Whoof Harted" or other such nomenclature.

Red's wife had lost her effectiveness at the bar and had moved to a corner of the tent away from the main conversation. This gave her the opportunity to drink more and forget life's disappointments. Irene had put on weight in recent years, but still had a well rounded figure. She wondered why a girl who loves it in any way possible has a husband who has grown tired of her and is openly fooling around with the sluts. As her eyes became heavier and her speech slower, she observed Stanley's guests and commented that at least they have each other, however little there was to have.

Several more key staff and invited guests had entered the tent and made their way to the bar. Red struggled to keep up with the requests for drinks, but it seemed impossible. Space was now at a premium, for only so many bodies will fit into a 20-by-20 tent. One effect of strong drinks is that soon nobody gives a damn. The party was rapidly approaching that stage, for the conversation was now reaching the shout level. With the music going full blast, the drinks flowing, and everyone comfortable, Stanley and Max slipped out to shower and dress and then move the party to the Tally-Ho.

The showers were located in the Mansion basement, under the kitchen. At one time there had been a drainpipe through this space, but when the showers were installed the pipe was cut off and left unused. The pipe still emptied into the shower, and it was a favorite joke to pour cold water on unsuspecting bathers.

"The party is really going great, Stanley."

"Yeah, I was glad to see my two gals make it. They should come through with about 25 bucks each for the week."

"That's a big tip. I don't get any that size."

"You never will, unless you find ways of letting guests know that for outstanding service, big tips are expected. They'll leave you practically nothing if you let them. I know, I've been here for nine years."

"Did you see the girl Al was with? She was fantastic."

"Yeah, but he'll make a fool of himself again and won't be able to do his work all week."

"You're probably right, Stanley, but she's sure a honey."

"He needs someone steady and stop all this fooling around. He's acting just like those little bastards on the ground crew, trying to screw everyone that he meets."

Stanley and Max had trouble getting the hot water adjusted. There seemed to be two options, scalding or lukewarm, with abrupt temperature changes each time water was used in the nearby kitchen. They had wanted to shower and dress as quickly as possible for the party. Even though it was the first big one of the season, everything was going great and the evening showed definite promise.

Then the shower went crazy. When a nearby commode flushed, Max immediately turned down the hot water and jumped back. Then someone turned on all the hot-water faucets in the kitchen sinks, and the shower went rapidly from scalding to cold to off—no pressure at all. Just as they were beginning to suspect that all of this was no accident, ice water came pouring out of the abandoned drainpipes. It had been years since such a trick had been played on Stanley. What idiot would dare do this to the headwaiter?

"I'll kill those bastards!" screamed Stanley as he grabbed his towel and ran from the showers for the basement stairs. Max was behind him yelling, "That goddamn ground crew did it." Max was so close behind him that when the basement lights suddenly went out and Stanley came to a startled halt, Max collided with him and they went down in a heap. They jumped right back up, ignoring their bruises, and continued their chase to the kitchen—where of course they found no one, and everything in order.

Their route to the kitchen took them through the chief cook's room, which was right next to the kitchen. Murphy came roaring out of bed, half asleep and half drunk on Irish whiskey. This must have seemed a nightmare to him—two raving, half naked waiters chasing through his bedroom late at night.

"You stupid bastards, what the hell are you doing here? Get the hell out! I'll have both of you fired! Crazy as hell, all of you!"

The Rex Robinson band started playing at 9 o'clock at the Tally-Ho. Every table had been filled early, for the girls knew from experience that an early start improved their chances of finding someone for the evening. At most dances the crowd gets loud and drunk as the night goes on, but at the Tally-Ho they *started off* loud and drunk. For many, the day had been a continuous drunk.

Dancing had started as soon as the recorded music began at 7 o'clock. There were a few couples on the floor, but most of the ladies were dancing with each other because of the shortage of men.

The Tally-Ho at one time had been a large stable. One wing had long, deep booths that had been horse stalls. They still carried the nameplates of horses, such as "Tosca" and "Arthur." The other wing was the dance area, which had been vastly enlarged over the years as the resort's crowds had grown. The connecting area was now a food counter and set-up area for drinks. All wings joined a cobblestone courtyard that was ideal for drinking in scenic surroundings. What had been the caretaker's living quarters over the stables now were separate dormitories for men and women. For $75 a week, a man or woman could get a bunk, meals, planned recreation, and perhaps even romance.

By the time the band had finished its first set of tunes, the dance floor was packed and would remain so until the last dance. The better dancers, mostly from New York City, requested the South American songs, for they could do the rumba, samba, and other Latin dances with expertise. As the evening advanced, the songs grew louder and faster.

Rand and I had slept through the staff meal, but ate in the kitchen. Murphy was now fully awake and in good spirits after the truck incident, and wanted to sing the Old Country songs. Both of us sang in the glee club at school, so Murphy was delighted to find a compatible soul—someone who could drink, sing, and share in a dislike of waiters. After a few drinks, it took little encouragement from Murphy, bent on revenge, to set up Stanley and Max's hot and cold shower.

Ann and Frances got to the dance early as they had planned, and expected Rand and I to be there waiting for them. When we didn't show after an hour, they joined a group of local guys. These were men who lived in the area and had purchased memberships that allowed them to participate in resort activities. Then when I did arrive I was with the Monk instead of Rand, whom Frances was interested in, so the girls decided to stay with the locals.

A few words about Monk here. Some men have style, some have class, but Monk has neither. Monk was a descendent of the French Huguenots who settled in the South Carolina low country, but he did not retain their religion or manners. And Monk definitely resembled a gargoyle. He had a wide jaw and bulldog-shaped face, with a mouth seemingly stretching from ear to ear. His teeth were stubby and irregularly spaced and his skin potted with acne scars. He bottomed out with a short, chubby body.

Monk was with me because Rand had kept his date with Janet for the movie, and I would otherwise be doing the evening alone. (Monk was sort of a temporary tag-along—you generally needed two to make out, since the girls usually traveled in pairs.) I was annoyed to find Ann with those other guys, but with four girls to each man here, why be pissed off? Make a good night of it and hope to score.

"Hi, I'm Claxton and this is my friend Monk. We're on the staff."

"I'm Mary Belanti and this is my friend Susie Chicavella. Are you waiters? Our waiter is Stanley, and he's terrific!"

"No, we work on the ground crew."

"Doing what?"

"Shoveling shit or whatever else nobody wants to do," grumbled Monk. The girls, a bit startled at his crude manner, quickly said goodbye and moved toward the courtyard.

"Why in the hell did you say that?"

"Because I didn't want to hear any more of that 'terrific waiter' bull. You begin to think that the waiters are the Chosen Ones—best money, best hours, best ass."

"Okay, let's try those two dancing together and don't tell them we're staff. Monk, you're going to have to show some class, or we'll never make out—I don't care how few men there are around here."

"Hi, where are you girls from?"

"We're from the City."

"What city?" asked Monk.

"*New York City*, of course, How about you guys?"

"I'm from Georgia and Monk's from South Carolina—the town of Ninety-six, to be exact."

"Well, I can see why you didn't know what 'the City' was."

"You New Yorkers certainly know how to dance good."

"Oh yes, people from the City are probably the finest dancers anywhere. Many of us dance almost every night, and we probably have more different places and bands than anywhere else."

"Well, would you like to dance with me?" asked Monk.

"Not really, you probably couldn't do the steps . . . being from the South."

"Well, that's alright," said Monk, once again wounded, "I've got to take a shit anyway." He disappeared into the crowd.

Muttering something unintelligible, the City girls turned and walked away.

I didn't realize how much I had drunk or how much it was beginning to show. After Monk made his exit I had two more bourbon and gingers with the kitchen crew, who were at a table in the corner.   The kitchen crew was permanent staff and lived locally.   Murphy had hired several boys just out of high school and trained them with a firm hand.   Dick Semanski was a cook and Bones Benkowski the baker.   Both did excellent work, and both hated waiters almost as much as Murphy did.

Maybe I should explain at this point why the waiters were so generally disliked by the kitchen staff.   The waiters were all college men in relatively easy and well paid jobs, having a ball for the summer.   They looked upon the kitchen hands as common workers who could do nothing else.   Hence, I had become a hero to the kitchen staff.

"Murphy told us that you knocked Max on his ass today," said Bones, gesturing for me to join them.

"I was just lucky to get in the first lick."

"Oh bullshit, you whipped his ass and everybody knows it.   Not only that, but they will never live down the way they got it in the shower tonight."

"How did you know about that?"

"Everybody knows about it.   You and Rand have become big men among the non-waiters."

"Does Mario know?"

"No, but if he did he would probably send you after Major O'Hara."

"Have you scored since you came here?" asked Bones.

"Almost."

"Well, Semanski and I think that heroes ought to be rewarded, and we're going to fix you up with a sure thing. See that girl dancing with Louie?   She's easy to make.   In fact, she'll put the make on *you*."   He was speaking of Louie Alpern, a waiter who worked in the staff dining room, and a fortyish looking bleached blonde he was dancing with.

The blond certainly didn't look all that appealing, but before I could get away from the table, she and Louie returned. She didn't look any better up close, but it was beginning to appear as if, for tonight anyway, it was her or nothing. At least I would be able to say I scored.

"Claxton, this is Gloria Kobowski. She can screw your ass off."

"That's the most flattering introduction I've ever had," she smiled, and seemed to appreciate my standing to acknowledge her arrival.

My experience with locker room language didn't quite prepare me for the sort of conversation that ensued. And Gloria was a drinker! She finished the drink Bones had fixed for her in a few long gulps, and was ready for a refill. I couldn't believe that anyone could drink so fast. Gloria certainly had the past-30 lush look—sagging chin and bags under her eyes. She was also losing the weight battle. However, those things didn't distress her as much as you might think. She had apparently decided at an early age that she didn't have to be slender or pretty to attract men; just give them what they wanted, and she could have all the attention she desired.

While Bones was pouring another round of drinks, I realized two things—I was getting very drunk and the dance would soon be over. Even with Gloria, I had to make some move in order to score, and time was running out.

Monk stumbled by the table with a drink in his hand. My dirty-mouth friend actually found someone who would dance with him—one of the New York girls! The friend of the one who had turned down my dance invitation. This one was a bit cross-eyed and obviously not as choosy about dance partners. She and Monk were now about danced out and were going to the old stall area for singing around the piano and some heavy drinking. Bones and Semanski joined them. They were nice enough to leave the bottle on the table, so the first order of making Gloria was to pour even more booze into her. I moved in closer, my leg pressing against hers, and placed my arm around her shoulder.

"You know, I always wanted to know someone like you."

"You mean you always wanted to *screw* someone like me."

"Yes, but you're such a good dancer, and you drink well and say what you think. Most girls I know fuss around and stall and make excuses as to why they can't, when all the time they want to."

"Really?"

"Just this afternoon Rand and I got drunk with two girls in their room. We wanted to shower with them, but they got all pissed off and threw us out."

"No kidding."

"Yeah, all we wanted was to shower, make love, and take a nap."

"Sounds great!"

"I'll bet *you* wouldn't throw us out."

"Oh no, I would have taken you in the shower, turned on the water real hot, soaped you all over, and held you close."

"Then what?"

"I would have taken you into the bedroom and screwed your brains out!"

I laughed and impulsively turned to kiss her, and was almost choked by her tongue going down my throat. I though I was passing out but was revived by her command of, "Let's dance."

If I had been sober, getting up with an erection to dance would have been embarrassing. The band was playing a slow moving, belly rubbing tune, and everyone was dancing as close as possible. Gloria gave me another deep French kiss.

"Let's go to my tent," I said.

"But honey, we've just begun to dance." She kept hunching and kissing me with her hands against my butt.

"Let's go to your car, then," I pleaded. But she kept on teasing.

"But I like to dance, and you said I'm a good dancer."

"You are, you are, but I've got a hard on and there are things I'd rather do than dance at the moment."

"You just said you liked me because I wasn't like other girls."

"Yes, that's right."

"You'd really like to go to bed with me, right?"

"Damn right, soon as we can!"

"Well," she said in a loud voice as she grabbed my crotch, "I'd like to too, but with *that* I don't think you could do me much good!"

The people around us had been picking up on our conversation and definitely heard the last remark, and there was general laughter when she made it. Don Williams, the social director, moved in to quiet things down.

"You'll have to leave the dance floor. We can't allow such behavior."

"What's the matter, do *you* want me too? I *know* you can't do anything. You're too afraid of Mario and your stupid job!"

Don led Gloria away and I faded sheepishly into the crowd. What a letdown! I thought I had a sure thing and she turned out to be a big tease. Maybe I try to be too nice to them!

I left the Tally-Ho shortly after the incident on the dance floor with Gloria and tried to find Monk, but my ground crew buddies were all in the stall area singing. Gloria had joined them and was singing "Ave Maria" at the top of her drunken voice. I decided to head back to my tent. The hill back to the staff tents was long and steep, no fun to climb under any circumstances but virtually impossible in my condition. I decided to stop and rest a bit right there on the ground.

"Wake up, you'll catch cold out here. Get up and come with me."

Half asleep, I realized that Ann had found me and was holding me up.

"Wake up! We'll get some coffee at the Carriage Room and you'll be alright."

"How did you get out here?" I asked.

"Escaping the local lovers who think you just shake hands and then fall in bed."

"How about Frances? Who did she end up with?"

"Some guy named Ken. He was a car nut and fascinated with the Mercury convertible. They left, and I just got tired of fighting off the guy I was with. Come on, let's get moving."

I was still shaky on my feet, but with her arm around my waist I began to return to the world of the living. The cool night air began to clear my head, and I realized that I was with someone who possibly cared about me.

Most of the dance crowd had left the Tally-Ho when the band stopped playing. They wanted to get to the

Carriage Room for a good seat—the Stumpers would be playing until 4:00 in the morning. We were about the last ones to walk up the hill. As we held each other tightly, we seemed to lose direction and just wandered toward the old Mansion.

The hill had been terraced down to the tennis courts which lay to the left of the Mansion. I stopped under the oak tree below the courts, needing to rest and feeling the urge to hold Ann close. Leaning back against the tree, I pulled her close to me. We kissed until I had to stop and take some deep breaths. My hands started running over her body.

"Not here, let's go to my room."

"Now, I can't wait."

"You've got to."

From the terrace side of the tennis courts came loud laughter.

"I don't believe it. That son of a bitch can really hump. Look at him go!"

As I looked up I saw a couple walking up the steps from the tennis courts, convulsed with laughter. The object of their merriment soon became apparent—lying on the ground were a man and woman wildly having sex. Monk, with his pants half off, was on top of Gloria, who was buck naked. They were both so drunk that they were oblivious to their public spectacle.

Then I was back at Ann's cabin for the second time. Her bed was narrow and her room cold. I had undressed immediately, but Ann hesitated. We lay on a red blanket with me naked and her dressed from the waist down.

My head was still spinning. I only remembered what a fool Gloria had made of me. Ann pulled my head between her breasts. At first I kissed then gently, but as she became more excited I began to suck and bite the nipples. My hands moved down her body, and she did not object when I loosened her slacks and pulled them off with her panties. Some people can't get an erection with too much to drink, but I was completely up and ready as she wrapped her leg around me and rubbed against my naked thigh.

"Get the rubber on now," she yelled, "before it's too late!"

But it was already too late.

Somehow I was in my bunk back at my tent when Monk came stumbling in.

"Claxton, wake me up at 6:45. I've got to drive some people to early mass."

"Where in the hell have you been, Monk? It's already 7:15."

"Oh, shit. Maybe there's a noon mass."

Chapter Five

 Angling for Better Jobs

The weekly staff meeting was held Monday mornings at 10 o'clock in the main dining room. Most guests had finished breakfast by that time, and the latecomers could eat at the breakfast bar or plan on an early lunch.

This Monday, the meeting helped Rand and me escape another lousy job. We had been patching the roof of the Mansion with hot tar. What made the roof work bearable was that it had so many gables that we could easily hide from Mike. You could even get in a little nap in the morning before it got too hot, but you had to make certain that you were braced against a chimney because there was always the danger of falling.

"Okay you guys, come on down. You can finish up this afternoon," yelled Mike from below. "It's time for the staff meeting; you're goofing off anyway."

"Was that son of a bitch really a first sergeant in the Army?"

"Naw, probably a frustrated corporal, wanting to be a sergeant. Look at him down there, strutting like a rooster."

"Yeah, especially with the staff girls around."

"Do you think he's got anything going with Terry?"

"Naw, I think she just plays him on so he'll help her with her work. It would be a perfect setup, though. He could be working on the plumbing as she cleans the room. They could make out, no questions asked."

"What I want to know is, what's a beauty queen doing working here as a maid? They say she represented Alabama at the Rose Bowl Parade last year."

"No shit."

"And what's a 40 year-old man doing in such a nothing job?"

As Rand and I came around the terrace to try to get a sweet roll and coffee from the breakfast bar, we were met by Mario rushing from his office to the meeting.

"Hi, Claxton, how are you enjoying your work?"

"Just fine, Mario."

"Is the food okay?"

"Certainly is, very good."

"How about the tents? Comfortable?"

"They're fine but a little cool early in the morning."

"Well, be sure to let the sides down at night and dress to keep warm. New England can be cool, but it could be worse. Where's your home, Claxton?"

"Georgia."

"I've been to Georgia several times to visit the battlefield at Kennesaw, near Atlanta."

I knew that Mario had something on his mind besides this general conversation, and it soon came out.

"Say, Claxton, I've noticed that 'Colonel' has been looking a little unkempt lately. Looks like he's been wallowing in some mud or something. Why don't you take time today to wash him good, and be sure to clean up his rear end so he will look good and fresh when the guests see him. Right now let's get to the staff meeting." He waved and headed on.

"Can you imagine that? I've become a dog's ass washer."

"You should have told him that you were from Virginia and that Robert E. Lee was your great grandfather. He'd have made you assistant director of the resort."

We were early enough to get a back row seat. The waiters always came in last, trying to give the impression that they were working hard and could not afford the time for the staff meeting.

"Hi gang," said Mario. "Now that the big part of the season is here, we have a few things to talk over. Claxton and several other people tell me that the staff food is very good. I want all of you to be well fed, and I told Murphy to serve the staff the same food as the guests, right Murphy?"

"Right, Mario."

"The season is getting into full swing, and we are depending on each of you to do a good job. You know that we have five applicants for each job, and you were chosen because we felt you were the best."

We applauded ourselves with faked enthusiasm.

"Now, as our guest list gets bigger and bigger, we need you on campus at night to help us entertain them. Many of the girls are very disappointed when they are not asked to dance, so let me tell you again, those of you who socialize with the guests will be rewarded with cash bonuses at the close of the season." He paused, looking out over the room.

"Now here comes another ass washing directive," said Rand.

"Yeah, when he starts looking off in a daze, he's up to something."

"Many of you have never really been away from home other than at college. I know it's difficult here when you have no one checking up on you, so some rules have to be made. It's easy to drink more than you need. We have had complaints from guests that some staff members have been too outgoing toward guests and have embarrassed them. We want you to have a good time here, but we can't afford a reputation like the White Horse Inn. That place, as you know, has become a non-stop orgy.

"One more item. Staff tent parties are fine, but they can't go on all night. Chief Day of our night security force told me that the girls in Tent Seven partied until 3 a.m., and after that some of the guests pulled the old trick of jacking up one side of the tent. We can't have that sort of thing—people can get hurt. Also, you can't stay up all night and do a good job the next day."

"Oh shit," I whispered, "back to the old curfew."

"Sounds like he's going to put us in chains."

"For your benefit and safety, I am making these rules: One: All tent parties will end by midnight. Two: All staff will be out of the public places by 1 a.m. unless you are off the next day. Stanley, do you have any comments?"

"Thank you Mario," said the headwaiter. "As you know, we encourage guests to know the staff and want them to be friendly with you, but the dining room is private for guests, and we cannot have staff walking through it as a shortcut to the lobby or pool. Also the breakfast bar is for guests who sleep late and miss breakfast, not for the staff who sleep late. Staff can only eat there on days off."

"Fuck you Stanley," came a whisper from the rear.

Old Syrup-Mouth pretended he didn't hear the remark, but his red face gave him away.

"One more thing. Everyone must help make the barbecue and Sunday buffet a success. It must all fit together. Mike's crew gets the fire ready, Murphy's crew prepares the food, and the waiters must serve it on time. The guests cannot be kept waiting to be served, so we must have the truck by 5 o'clock to move the food to the pine grove. Staff will be served immediately after guests, but not before all guests are served. If you're late without an excuse, then you've missed dinner."

"Thank you, Stanley. Murphy, do you have any comments?"

"Yes, Mario," said the head cook. "Staff must eat in the staff dining room at the hours posted, except when meals are missed because of working. Then you can eat in the kitchen after all guests have been served."

"No staff is to come into the kitchen except on business. State health laws prohibit this unless you have a health card. We can have no more clowning, jokes, pranks, or monkey business such as pouring cold water in the staff showers as happened Saturday night."

A sudden burst of wild laughter, stomping, and applause from all the staff except the waiters caused Murphy to break into a wide smile as he sat down.

Stanley was stone-faced and visibly embarrassed as he whispered to Max, "We'll get those bastards."

"Okay, gang," said Mario, "we've got a lot of work ahead of us, so let's try to follow the rules. All of you know Mike who is in charge of maintenance."

Mike addressed the most urgent maintenance problem of the moment.

"Chambermaids should be sure to tell the guests not to put their used Kotex in the commode. We've worked all morning unstopping a john in the Mansion, and you know the mess we have when a john runs over on the third floor dormitory."

"We know his job now. The keeper of the johns," said Rand.

"Two more things that cause problems. One is that you cannot hang laundry in the boiler room to dry. If the fire marshal found laundry there, he would lay a heavy fine on Handover. Also, will the lovers who are using the storage room please move to the pine grove." This, of course, drew a few laughs.

"And one more thing, the tents cannot be heated because of the fire hazard. You must keep the side flaps down and dress for cool weather."

"Thank you, Mike. And now Mrs. Cicarelli, our housekeeper."

"Some of you have not turned in your linen on time. As posted, you can pick up clean linen on Tuesday from 10:00 until 11:30 in the morning. Jerry Wise will handle this and keep the records. So far we have some staff members who have not changed their linen in a month."

"Monk's linen is so dirty they'll never get it clean," I whispered to J.T. "Did you know he threw up on it last night?"

"Our last supervisor is Don Williams, and then we'll move to the south terrace for our annual staff picture. Take it away, Don."

"With the season in full swing we must have more activities for the guests. All of you were hired because you had some sort of athletic ability or extra talent. The guests are enjoying the softball games with our staff team four times a week. We'd also like to develop a basketball team to play three times a week. We need someone to assist Sara, our tennis instructor. We also need a full time person at the pool, for maintenance and to direct pool activities. Let me know if you are interested. Also, see Stanley about dancing with the exhibition square dance team. You'll enjoy that, and practicing will get you off work a little."

"The fashion show was a great success, and I want to thank each of you who worked on it. Mike's crew did a great job, as did all the girls who modeled the clothes. We were written up in the *Times* as one of the better shows on the fashion tour of the resorts."

"Thank you, Don, and if any of you want to be on the Thursday night amateur show, get lined up with Bob Glass for a tryout. Jenny Cook is doing a good job singing, and Bob Laney's magic show is great. Remember, those of you who take part in these activities will also get a bonus at the end of the season. Okay, everybody, out to the south terrace for our picture."

"That was the shortest meeting we've ever had," said Rand.

"Too short. I had hoped it would last until lunch; then we could relax on the roof while Mike finishes the plumbing job."

"Aw shit, he's not working; he's just looking for an excuse to screw around with Terry."

"And, I think we should look into the tennis and pool job. The pay's no better, but we'd have a greater chance to be with the women and find something before the waiters move in."

"What do you know about tennis, other than the little you played at school?"

"Look, I played on my high school team and won the junior city championship. I probably could have played somewhere in college, but so few schools have tennis scholarships. Anyway, I know I can teach beginning tennis, especially to good looking gals."

"Do you think you can work with Sara? She seems like a bitch to me."

"She just taught gym classes too long. I think she hates all women. I'll let her teach the men, and I'll teach the women. After teaching high school gym classes all year, she should be glad to have the assistance of a young, energetic male like me."

"You're a dreamer. She'll make a slave out of you. All she wants is someone to do the dirty work like keeping the courts in shape. That means starting at 7:30 every morning with watering, rolling, and sweeping them before 9 o'clock when her lessons begin."

"But wouldn't you like to get away from Mike and that damn ground crew? As long as we're there, we'll get the same old shitty jobs, like working the drainage field and washing the dog's ass. I'm going to see Williams about it, and I think you should get the pool job. Monk and J.T. got those driving jobs, so why can't we get something better? Fuck Mike. He can find someone else for his dirty work."

"Okay, we'll see him at lunch."

The meeting with Williams went very well. He remembered that Rand and I had worked our asses off until midnight at the fashion show. He said we could have the jobs if Sara wanted us.

That damn fashion show had really screwed up my last night with Ann. I had counted on a big evening with her, but the show lasted so late that she got pissed off, and we wound up having a miserable time. She had planned to come back up in two weekends, but after Saturday I doubt that she will. The more I think about it, the more I realize how much this job stinks. One thing is certain, though. I can meet more girls teaching tennis than I can putting hot tar on the roof or working a sewage drain field.

"Claxton, Rand, get out of those bunks and get that job finished on the Mansion roof."

"Aw shit, doesn't that guy ever take a nap after lunch?"

"No, he gets us back to work, then he slips off for a nap while working on the plumbing. I'll still bet he's banging Terry."

"Well, let's get back to it. I hope this will be my last day with him. Sara wants me to hit with her after dinner so she can tell if I know enough about tennis to help her."

The afternoon temperature had reached the mid-eighties, but the roof temperature was near a hundred. Rand and I wanted to make this job last all afternoon, but the heat and odor of the tar made it impossible. I really had two great choices—swelter on a smelly roof or wash the dog's ass as Mario had directed.

"Rand, did I ever tell you about the tennis trip we made down to Emory in Atlanta after baseball ended?"

"You just mentioned that it was pretty wild; that several of you were drinking laboratory alcohol that Dr. Oldfield supplied."

"Right. That's why he was fired, but that's not the whole story. We lost the match real bad, and started home after eating at Emory's dining hall. Two of the senior players were veterans and wanted to stop for a beer. Dr.

Oldfield had a quart of pure alcohol, and the three of them started drinking it with Coca-Cola."

"Did you drink any?"

"Not at first, but as they began to get high—and that didn't take long—I drank some too. It sure packed a wallop—I couldn't talk after two drinks!"

"Who drove the car if Dr. Oldfield was getting drunk?"

"Steve Park and Jim Olson didn't drink, so Jim drove the car."

"Is that all that happened?"

"Oh, no. As we got close to Athens, Dr. Oldfield became very talkative. He raved about how many college girls he had screwed and how many times he had been to Effie's cathouse near Athens. He even talked about Dr. Cook in the education department, and how she used to lay everybody on campus."

"That doesn't surprise me. I knew some guys who say they screwed her at her house last summer. I'd like to take her course and fuck my way to a passing grade."

"Anyway, Park got all excited about the Effie talk and suggested that we visit her place. Drunk as I was getting, I still couldn't believe that Dr. Oldfield went along with the idea. Not until we pulled up in front of the place."

"Hot damn! Did you score?"

"Shut up, let him tell the story."

"It was an old house in a run-down neighborhood. Effie greeted Dr. Oldfield like an old friend. I couldn't believe what I was seeing—about six girls in a sitting room playing cards, and all wearing just house coats. While Dr. Oldfield and Effie talked on about old times, Ed Ross grabbed one of the girls and disappeared. My mind was a little blurred, but I was certain I could do what Ross had done. I was stupid enough to ask where they had gone, and one of the girls came over and whispered, "For five dollars I'll show you."

"I don't believe that. Only five dollars?"

"This is what you might have trouble believing. Dr. Oldfield came over, gave me a five, and told me to have a good time."

"Maybe he was returning the same sort of gift to him when he was a sprite. Then what?"

"She led me downstairs to a bedroom and got undressed in about 10 seconds. Man, she had big tits and a beautiful body. She had this big scar from her naval down to her cunt. I didn't know then, but found out from Dr. Oldfield that it was probably caused by a Caesarean section.

"She then took my five and stuck it in a drawer and began to undress me. I was ready for anything when she was leaning down to untie my shoes. I later realized that she wanted to get through as quickly as possible and get on to someone else. She got pissed off when I got up to get a rubber. I had been carrying it in my wallet for a month, and I had been told to always use one with a whore to keep from getting the clap or something."

"How was it?"

"Very disappointing. I was about to come by the time we got on the bed. She had teased me, and as she was putting it in I was already coming."

"Well, that was what you would call a real quickie."

"I call it a waste of five dollars, but that wasn't the end of it. She got dressed as quickly as she undressed and had me back upstairs to face Dr. Oldfield, who immediately labeled me 'rabbit'."

"What happened to Ross and his girl?"

"This was unbelievable. In about 30 minutes she came screaming up the stairs with Ross trying to pull her back down. What he did to her was never discussed, but it must have been pretty awful, even for a cathouse! Effie grabbed Ross and slapped the hell out of him. Dr. Oldfield, Bob and I had to keep Ross off Effie because she was calling the police. Dr. Oldfield finally got her settled down, and we got out of there. It scared the hell out of me. I thought we would all be in jail before the night was over."

"Hey, you guys, how much longer are you going to take on that job?" came Mike's voice from the terrace.

"We'll need most of the afternoon to finish."

"Save it for tomorrow. I need you for another job. Come on down."

I explained that Mario had told me to wash the dog, so Mike took Rand to the pool to help fix some problem they were having with the pumping equipment.

Washing the dog wasn't nearly as bad as I had expected. Colonel was a five-year-old collie who didn't like the idea of being washed, but made only a couple of attempts to get out of the tub before submitting to the unpleasant experience.

I had finished my dinner early and gone back to the tent to get dressed in my tennis clothes for the match with Sara. My tennis shoes were shot. I had last worn them the day we worked in the septic drain field. They were still muddy, but would have to do since you weren't allowed to play on the clay courts with anything but smooth-soled shoes. My only tennis shirt had roof tar on it, so I was all set to make a real impression on Sara.

She was waiting for me on the back courts. I was worried that she would want to play on the courts by the Mansion terrace, and all the guests would see us as they left the happy hour for dinner. I wanted a chance to practice a little before going on display.

Sara was friendly, but meant business. In the warm-up I hit two balls on the frame of my racquet and they sailed over the back fence. This certainly didn't impress her since she had opened a new can of balls, and one of them was lost. As we hit a few more I gradually regained my timing and began hitting the ball in the center of the racquet. After we hit for about 30 minutes she walked over to the low wall surrounding the court and sat down.

"How much tennis have you played?"

"I started playing at fourteen in the public park. I never had any lessons except the coaching I got in high school. Tennis was never big in Savannah, so most of my playing was at the public courts."

"Did you ever play in tournaments?"

"Yes, the state high school and city championship tournaments."

'How did you do?"

"I never did too well in the state high school tournaments. I would win a match or two and then have to play somebody from Atlanta. They were always pretty good, and I lost to them; but I did win the Savannah junior city tournament.

"I can tell you haven't played much lately, but you do have good strokes, and you move well. Those are the things that make a good player. When you won the Savannah tournament, did you beat any strong players? For example, anyone out of state or ranked very high?"

"Only in the finals."

"How did you beat him?"

"Have you ever been in a Southern coastal city in mid-August?"

"No. Pretty hot, I guess."

"We played the match at 3:00 in the afternoon in 98 degree weather and 95 percent humidity. My opponent, a guy named Chuck Daniels, was on the tennis team of Baylor Academy in Chattanooga. He was top seeded in the tournament and I was seeded fourth, so he was definitely favored to win. In fact he walked away with the first set, 6-love. He had practiced with the pro before the match and was really sharp. His parents and friends were there, and they felt certain Chuck would win easily since he had been in school for the summer and had played a lot of tennis. His game was great, but he wasn't as conditioned as I was to the steamy weather in Savannah that time of year. He won the first set because I tried to hit with him, and I figured at that point that my only chance was to play the return game—you know, lobs, underspins, make him run and work for every point. My strategy worked—the heat began getting to him in the second set, which I won 6-3, and he completely collapsed in the third set, which I won 6-1.

"That's smart tennis. If you can use your head like that here, you can definitely help me with the tennis program."

"What's expected of me in this job?"

"My main problem is that I have more people than I can work with. Most of them are beginners, and I just can't get to everybody for individual instruction. Some of them are so dumb they can't work in a group, and they expect to learn in a week. Mario is on me to be sure they get instruction, or at least think they have, so they will want to come back. I need you to work with the very beginners in basic strokes and to get them started, while I work with those who have played and are more advanced. After teaching physical education during the school year, I'm fed up with working with beginners."

"Williams told me I would also be responsible for keeping up the courts."

"That's true. Regular maintenance just hasn't worked out—Mike won't get his crew here early enough. Most mornings they are still working on the courts while I'm trying to give lessons. Mario has taken the maintenance responsibility away from him and turned it over to me."

"I know the guys who worked on the courts for Mike, and they certainly didn't like the work."

"Mario is aware that the courts must be maintained and has told me to get somebody dependable."

"Sara, if you start your lessons at 10 o'clock, what time will I have to start getting the courts ready? I hope not 7 o'clock or thereabouts."

"You can start at 8:00 or 8:30 and get done in time easily once you learn how to do it. All that's needed is to wet the courts down at night and roll and sweep them the next morning."

"Let me suggest this. Rand wants the job working on the pool, so why not let us work together. He could help me in the morning on the courts, and I'll help him with the pool in the afternoon."

"That suits me fine, but you'll have to be ready for tennis instruction at 2:00 in the afternoon as well as 10:00 in the mornings. You and Rand be here at 8:00 tomorrow morning and I'll show you what needs to be done. Right now, I'm going to have a drink. Want to join me?"

"Not today, I've got to find Rand and get our tent straightened out. Mario gave us hell yesterday when he saw some wicker chairs we'd taken from the Mansion basement, and also because our tent was a general mess. So we've got to get things straightened out by tomorrow or be restricted."

"Okay. We'll have that drink another time."

By the time I got back to the tent, Rand had cleaned up his area and had gone to the movies with Janet. Maybe Rand had the right idea, dating someone on the staff. Janet seemed to be very pleasant, but the only time I ever saw her was at lunch. She and Jenny would always come late for lunch, which the staff really appreciated because the girls smelled like the horse stables where they worked. She must have to take long showers at night.

Monk and J.T. had their own evenings ruined when they had to drive some guests to the dance festival, so for the first time in a month I had a chance to get to bed early. I got the rest of the tent halfway cleaned and most of the clothes off the floor and headed for the shower. My "robe" was an old raincoat without buttons that I found among some junk at the resort. As I passed Tent One, a party was just breaking up and people were headed for the Tally-Ho. They were finishing their last "Betwixt the Sheets" and "Whoof Harteds" and were in good spirits. I was trying to see who had been at the party and stumbled in a hole in the road. I dropped my towel, soap, and toothbrush as I tried to catch my balance, and the old raincoat opened, exposing me to the world and to the people leaving the party. Their laughter followed me in my rapid flight to the showers. My hope was that it was too dark for any to recognize me.

I couldn't believe I was getting to bed at 10 o'clock. Not since the basketball season at Coyee College had I gone to bed so early. It was hard to get my mind settled, though, like the nights after the games when I would still be awake at daybreak replaying the game, especially if we had lost.

How could anyone sleep when there was so much going on, so much fun to be had, but still I had to be ready for Sara and the new job. I tried to relax and get some sleep.

Just as I started to drift off, the door of the tent opened and some—no, two people!—groped their way toward J.T.'s bed.

"Do you want me to turn on the light?"

"No, somebody might see me, and I can't afford that."

"Come on, then, let's lay on the bed so we can be comfortable."

The woman didn't seem to be all that eager about what she was doing.

"I'm not too sure about this, even though the bastard's got it coming. He ignores me and screws those stupid nurses." I recognized her voice—Irene, the wife of Red Kelly.

"Don't worry, baby, you're with me now and I'll treat you right."

"I want to, but I'm afraid—suppose he finds out?"

"He won't find out unless you tell him."

There followed some petting sounds—heavy breathing, twisting and turning on the bunk.

"No, don't open my blouse. I know he did me wrong, but what would he do if he found out?"

"Look baby, I don't have much time; I've got to drive back to town to pick up some people at the theater."

"I'm sorry, I thought I could but I can't. I've never done this before, and I feel so guilty. I've got to go before it's too late."

"Don't go. Just let me love you and do what you like."

"No, I can't. I love him, and I've got to find him. Let me go now, please."

"Well, why in the hell did you come in here? Why did you lead me on? You prick teaser!"

"I don't know, but please let me go. Please, please understand."

"Oh, get out and go fuck yourself, you dumb bitch!"

She disappeared as quickly as she had appeared. I lay still, hoping that J.T. would leave without turning on the light, but as he stood up with his eyes adjusted to the darkness, he saw my shape in the top bunk.

"Damn! You heard everything! What the hell are you doing here so early?"

"Just trying to get some sleep. Sorry you didn't make out."

"Shit! Don't tell anybody about this. That woman made me look dumb."

"I won't. I wasn't trying to spy. I figured the worst thing I could do was to let her know I was here."

"It pisses me off," he said. "This is about the fifth time I've almost scored, but didn't. Something like this always happens. All the excuses—I'm not that kind of girl, or I'll get pregnant, or you won't love me if I do that. They get you hot, then suddenly stop."

"Same with me, J.T. That damn Gloria put it to me last Saturday night at the dance.

"Yeah, I heard about it."

"But worst of all, Monk screwed her later."

"That damn Monk is just lucky. I try to be nice to someone and get nothing; he treats them like dirt, and they drop their drawers for him."

"How did you meet this girl?" I asked.

"She had been at the Tent One party and was walking down to the Tally-Ho, completely stoned. I was driving in from town and offered her a ride. She rode back to town with me and got real friendly in the car, so I brought her to the tent."

I pretended I didn't know who the woman was.

"Well, who was she? I heard her say something about hurting him."

"I can't tell you that. I was sure I had it made."

"Well, I guess this proves that there is no sure thing."

"Oh, to hell with all of it. When we came up here I thought you could score every night. It's no better than school, only here I work every night."

"One thing's for sure—you're not going to find anything unless you get out and look for it. I had planned to go to bed early, but I think this might be the night I've waited for."

"I'll see you later. I've got to pick up the people who went to the summer stock theater at Stockbridge."

"You know, J.T., I'm so tired every day that I just don't know if I can make it or not. Like today when Rand and I were working on the roof, I needed a nap so bad that I crawled up against the chimney and slept 15 minutes. But when the sun goes down I come alive, and I'm headed for the Tally-Ho as soon as I get dressed. You know, a good time is out there and I don't want to miss it."

Chapter Six

 Fine Wine and Yvonne

I was surprised to find the crowd at the Tally-Ho much smaller and quieter than on my Saturday visit, and later found out that was true of weeknights. But Mario was just as busy, making sure that male staff members were dancing with the girls who had no partners.

Because the crowd was smaller than on my last visit, the preponderance of females was clearly in evidence. The ratio of available female to male guests seemed to be about four to one. While this created a most interesting situation for me and the other men, the truth was that most of the girls were ordinary looking at best. Here and there were a few good lookers scattered among the tables. What made it bad for the ordinary looking girls early in the season was that nearly all of the guys pursued the good lookers. As the weeks went by, however, the staff guys wised up. They learned that the more attractive girls weren't quite as eager as the others. The good lookers liked to dance and be seen, but usually that was all. The ordinary girls were more appreciative of your attention.

No sooner had I made my entrance than Mario hurried over to me. I knew what was coming—go dance with the homelies—so I made a dash for a dark corner table. It turned out to be the Tent One group, and to my surprise I was invited to join those elite folk. The group included only two girls, but both were attractive. One, in fact, was a knockout, up there in the Elizabeth Taylor class. She had light colored eyes and coal black hair that hung down over her shoulders . . . and what I could see of her figure was very nice. Since none of the other guys seemed to be rushing her, and she directed a nice smile in my direction, I wasted no time.

"Hi, I'm Claxton. Would you like to dance?"

"My my, the Flasher himself!"

"Oh no! You saw that! How did you recognize me in the dark?"

"I didn't, but you were pointed out as you came in."

"I'm sure I provided a lot of laughs for the Tent One crowd."

"You did indeed, and may have a new nickname for awhile."

"The Flasher—that's a name sure to get attention! But maybe not the kind I want." I looked at her thoughtfully and impulsively blurted out, "I've been looking for a girl like you all summer. One who might get interested in me too."

She was just as forthright: "Well, you've met a girl who is interested in you."

"Do you really mean that? I thought all I've done is provide you with a few laughs—you and the Tent One crowd you've been socializing with."

"I've decided that anyone who the waiters dislike as much as you has to be an interesting person."

"I guess they have their reasons for not liking me."

"Did you really do all the things they accuse you of—like stealing the truck and then beating up poor Max or throwing cold water on Stanley while he was in the shower?"

"If you believe all of that, you certainly have been brainwashed. Maybe I should go on and leave you with them. Ya'll can have a few more laughs at my expense."

"Please don't go. I want you to stay and dance with me."

"Do you mean it? I'm honored—you're certainly the most beautiful belle at the ball."

"Why thank you, sir. I would act more Southern, but I'm from New York City—East 82nd Street, to be exact."

"What difference would that make?"

"I thought Southern men liked helpless women, not us know-it-all New York types."

"Southern men like beautiful women from anywhere."

"Let's dance before that dull bunch of waiters returns to the table."

"Who are you with?"

"No one, but Fran Mitchell keeps trying to move in on me. He thinks he's Mister Adonis, the world's most beautiful man. What a jerk!"

"How did you get involved with the Tent One crowd?"

"I'm not involved, but they play the one-up game, or whatever you want to call it. Everyone makes being invited to the Tent One parties the major event of the week. Once invited, you are then with the 'in' group."

"Who makes it such a big deal?"

"They do."

"But how?"

"Stanley sets you up like this. He will ask the people at the next table if they are coming when he already knows they are not. He gets your attention by giving an elaborate, detailed description of what takes place—how much fun they have and who was there."

"So what?"

"Everyone wants to meet new people, get in on the fun. They make you think that Tent One has it all."

"You don't act too excited about being invited, but what do they do?"

"Only somebody really stupid would fail to see through them."

"Yes, we have plenty of stupid people here, but what do they do?"

"They hustle drinks on you, complain about how hard they work, and try to butter you up for a big tip when they leave. In the meantime, old Fran and the others try to feel you up and take anything else they can from you."

"And do the girls usually give in to them?"

"Sometimes, I guess, but I didn't. Really, they are the dullest people I've ever been around. Stanley's act is the best of all. He tells about how tough veterinarian school is and how hard he works at the clinic. I couldn't take it. You're a welcome relief, even if you are the 'Flasher'."

"Stanley is known as 'Old Syrup Mouth' with that phoney drawl. But to hell with him. Let's just have a good time."

"That's the best offer I've had lately."

"May I have this dance, mademoiselle?"

"Mai oui, but how did you know I'm French?"

"You look exactly as a French girl should—beautiful, exciting, daring—and I also heard your friend say she would be back shortly, 'Yeavonne.'"

"No, no, the name is Yvonne, with the y pronounced *e*."

"Well, it sounds Southern French anyway."

"To get back to your earlier question, yes I would like to dance but somewhere quiet with French wine and soft music."

I happen to have heard of such a place, but we'll need transportation. Do you have a car?"

"No, not here. I came by train."

"I'll see what I can do about a car after we dance. For now, let's dance and get away from this table."

As we moved to the dance floor and she relaxed in my arms like a beautiful dream, I knew that I wasn't going to let her get away. The band had gotten loud, and the crowd was getting noisier as the evening wore on. This just wasn't the place to entertain a beautiful French girl from New York. Besides, Fran had discovered that I had taken her away from their table. He was waiting to grab her and try to embarrass me.

"Yvonne, I just don't like this music tonight. I think we would enjoy some quiet place more. If I stay with you here, Fran is going to make a scene, so why don't we leave now?"

"That's fine with me. I can't take much more of this loud music, and I definitely will not go back to the Tent One table."

"You go to the ladies' room, and I'll get us a car."

Fran tried to stop her as she was leaving the dance floor. I couldn't hear what she said, but he got the message. He looked really pissed and started in my direction. I took the coward's way out by making a quick exit out the side entrance and got lost in the crowd in the Tally-Ho annex that used to be the stables. Why ruin a promising evening with a confrontation with an ex-marine?

Monk had been driving a group to the summer stock theater, and was now in the stable bar with the sing-in group. It sounded wild, but I needed a car badly and Monk might be crazy enough to let me have the station wagon.

"Hey Monk, you're through driving early tonight, aren't you?"

"Yeah, J.T. is driving the late crowd back—the ones who wanted to stay in Stockbridge for a drink."

"Monk, I want to ask a favor of you. Do you have to turn in the keys to the station wagon after you get back?"

"I'm supposed to turn them in at the front desk, but most of the time I keep them. But what's the favor? As if I'm not beginning to suspect."

"Could you let me have the station wagon for a couple of hours to take a good looking girl out?"

"I'm not driving the station wagon. Mike has it."

"What are you driving?"

"Mario's car—the Chrysler New Yorker."

"Aw shit, then you can't let me have it."

"I didn't say that. I said I wasn't driving the station wagon."

"You mean you would let me have the Chrysler?"

"I'm not letting you have anything, but it's parked in front of the Mansion with the keys in it. Mario will drive it home after he leaves the Carriage Room about 3 o'clock, so be sure to have it back by then or plan to head South tomorrow."

Yvonne was sitting in the snack bar smoking a cigarette in a fancy holder. She looked terrific, and several guys nearby looked like they were ready to make their move. I realized that I had lucked into something really nice. Here I was with a beautiful, intelligent woman whom I had rescued from a dull evening. Maybe I should change my approach—be less aggressive and let her take the initiative. Why not let her do what she would like while I play Mr. Nice Guy and wait and see. The one thing I should have learned here is that the girl decides what finally happens. The car situation was risky, but some guys, and me in particular, would do anything to please this beautiful woman.

"Would you like to wait here while I get the car from the Mansion?"

"I'm ready to leave any possible way. The wolves here are just too much."

I got the feel of the car as we drove the dirt road to the highway, then gunned the motor as we entered the highway. Yvonne seemed to love the drive and was even more exciting with the wind blowing through her hair. She never asked where I got the car.

"Would you rather take the quick route through town or the long, scenic drive?"

"I see a city every day. Tonight I want to enjoy the world I don't see enough of. Let's take the scenic route."

The faster I drove the more she seemed to like it. I wanted to talk, but the noise from the wind and tires on the road made that impossible. Besides, she seemed lost in her thoughts, and I felt she would let me share those thoughts at the time of her choosing.

We had gone 20 miles out of the way around the belt expressway at a speed of over 80 most of the time. I finally had to slow down to make the turnoff at the Blendtyre exit.

"Well, here's the exit to the place I told you about," I said.

"I could drive on forever. It gives me the feeling of escape—complete freedom. It takes me back to a world of long ago."

The turnoff road was paved for about a mile, and then we were in New England countryside. I had read about New England birches and mending walls as written by Robert Frost, but he didn't describe them on a moonlit night with a beautiful girl. Yvonne moved close to me as we drove slowly on the dirt road, put her arm around me, and gently kissed my cheek.

"Thank you for rescuing me."

"Rescuing you from what?"

"From a dull evening, and making me happier than I've been in a long time. Even if it ended now I would be completely satisfied."

"Not me . . . but I hope I can enjoy that sort of fulfillment before the evening is over."

"Let's see what happens."

We arrived at our destination. Blendtyre, like Handover, had been the estate of a rich New Yorker. The owners had made it a very exclusive restaurant some years ago. It had been a favorite of Koussevitzky, the famous conductor, and had increased in popularity along with his Tanglewood festival. The stone walls that lined the circular entrance gave it New England charm, but it was almost a replica of Jefferson's Monticello at Charlottesville. I wasn't sure that we could get in, but I heard that Stanley went there often, and that using his name would get you a table. We were met by a black maitre d'hotel.

"Good evening, sir. Do you have reservations?"

"No, but I was told by Stanley at Handover to tell Roosevelt Jones that I was a good friend of his, and that he would get me a table."

"Oh, yes, Stanley is one of my best friends in the City. We're filled, but I'll get you in. Would you like a table on the terrace?"

"I would like that, if it isn't too cool for the lady."

"We'll take it, Roosevelt. Claxton will have to keep me warm."

I was disappointed in the layout of the terrace, which was very small with the tables almost touching. But the scenery was superb.

"This view is just gorgeous, Roosevelt. Thank you so much."

"We try hard to please the ladies, especially when they are as pretty as you, miss. He's here because of you, and don't let him forget that."

"Oh my, you're very nice. Are you really from New York?"

"Heavens no, I'm from Gainesville, Florida. I was stationed at Fort Dix in New Jersey with the Army, and just stayed in New York after I was discharged. Stanley and I work together at an animal clinic. Now, what can I get you?"

"We're not real hungry, but would like something light with French wine."

"We stopped serving dinner at 11 o'clock, but have a midnight supper for people who would like to eat light after the symphony. I'll get the menu."

"Oh Claxton, this is just beautiful."

"I thought you would like it."

"You probably bring all of your girlfriends here."

"No, it's the first time."

Is that Mount Greylock in the distance?"

"I think so. Looks different from this direction."

"Then those must be the White Mountains. Have you been to Williamstown yet?"

"No, I haven't been anywhere. This is the first time I've left Handover at night except for one movie. Mario wants all the staff to stay on campus to help entertain guests."

"You should see Williams College. It's a very fine private school. Where do you go to school?"

Roosevelt returned with menus before I could answer, but that was fine with me. I wasn't interested in school talk tonight.

"Let me know when you are ready to order, but may I suggest the Coquille, St. Jacques."

"How about the wine list?" asked Yvonne.

"It's on the inside of the menu."

"Thank you, Roosevelt."

"This selection of French wine is excellent," she said. "I would like to taste all of them. What is your favorite?"

"I'm afraid my knowledge of wine is too limited to make a good selection."

"Do you want a brief description of each?"

"I'd rather just trust your judgment."

"I'll try not to disappoint you. I suggest that we select a dry, white wine—something light that goes well with any food, but I really am not hungry. Roosevelt, I think we will have the Piesporter Riesling and just skip the food." As he bowed and left, she turned to me.

"Claxton, you could not have found a more beautiful place in all of New England for drinking good wine."

"It reminds me of the mountains of north Georgia, but this is much cooler."

"Did I tell you that I was born in France?"

"No, you didn't tell me much of anything about yourself except that you've had a lousy time at Handover."

"That's very true, until tonight. But I did spend my childhood in France."

Roosevelt returned, much more quickly than I thought he would.

"Here is your wine, sir. I think it will please you."

"Do I have to go through that tasting bit, Roosevelt?"

"It's customary for all good wines, sir."

"Forget the 'sir' stuff, Roosevelt. Anyway, it tastes great, and thank you."

"I hope you enjoy it, my Southern friend and beautiful lady."

After he left, Yvonne stared at me intently. I sensed that an important question was coming.

"Do you know what day this is?"

"Well, let's see, it's the second week of July or the third—it's Monday, July 14th, and if my history is correct, this is Bastille Day."

"You're correct! But a Frenchman would say 14th of July, and the first toast of tonight is to Paris—may she live another two thousand years!"

"I'll drink to that."

"The wine is excellent, but the company is even better. It's been so long since I've enjoyed such a lovely place. Why don't we just stay here all night and drink wine?" she asked.

"We'll stay here as long as you like. The wine goes down so easily and tastes so good."

"Be careful, now. Wine can slip up on you before you know it, and then I'll have to do the driving home."

"I can handle it, but can you?"

"Being French, I was raised on wine, but I have great respect for it. Show caution with that second glass. Nurse it along and enjoy it to the fullest, as you would the company of a stimulating companion."

"This stuff is great. Why haven't I discovered it before this?"

"I haven't been in the South, but I've read that drinking of alcohol there isn't approved of except in the large cities. So you see, you have missed the great pleasure of enjoying fine wines."

"But not the pleasure of beautiful women."

"Are there any beautiful women at your school?"

"A few, but they always seem to be taken. The older guys get their pick, and underclassmen have to take what's left. How about your school? Were there many men?"

"We had very little social life. Everyone tried to excel in studies. There was no student housing, so everyone lived at home, which pretty well eliminated most social situations."

"Didn't you have any sports programs?"

"Oh no, we were purely academic. Everyone attended classes and did research. We were taught that excellence through studies was the only road to success. Pour me more wine; I want to forget those studies tonight and enjoy living."

"What has all this academia gotten you?"

"A research position, graduate school, and more disciplined study. I wish I could have taken more time to enjoy my undergraduate days."

"You mean you already have your degree?"

"I have my M.S. in chemistry and a year of research study."

"Damn, how could you do all that and be—what, twenty-one at the most?"

"It started years ago. My mother came from a professional family. Her father was a doctor and her mother a college professor. They brought my mother up very strict and properly educated. She, too, married a doctor. Mother was determined that I would have a strict upbringing also, but my father did not agree. He wanted me to be a happy child more than anything else, and I was while he lived. The drive over here brought back memories of the Moselle River region of France where we lived."

"What part of France is that?"

"It's on the German border of what they call Alsace, which used to be part of Germany but was returned to France after the first World War. Actually the wine is German, as you can tell from the label. Piesporter means it's from the town of Piesport, and Riesling is the best German wine grape. If it were the *best* Piesporter, it would have the vineyard name on it. I chose it because I knew it would be light and dry and not bitter."

"It's good. I can't believe we've finished the bottle so quickly, but we can always order more." I beckoned to Roosevelt and ordered another bottle, figuring that even if they cost something like five bucks each, this evening was worth it.

"Were you still in France during the war?"

"Yes, being on the border we were overrun by the Germans in the first week of fighting. My father was killed while treating the wounded, so after France fell we went to Paris to live with my grandparents."

"I'll bet the occupation was awful."

"It was. There was severe food and other rationing, and then after two years my grandparents were caught aiding the underground. They were put in prison and we heard in 1943 that they had died. My mother and I had a very difficult time finding food and shelter until Carl came along."

"Now who was Carl?" But first let me pour you more Piesporter from the Moselle section of France, made from Riesling grapes. See how fast I learn!"

"Very good, you will know one good wine if you are alive tomorrow. Now about Carl. He had worked as a chef in some of the most famous hotels in Europe, including Berlin. When the German generals learned of his experience, they made him their exclusive chef. My mother had known Carl as the son of their family cook. I think he had been very fond of her when they were children. How they met in Paris I don't know, but he supplied us with food, and my mother married him."

"This wine is the best I've ever tasted," I said. Why didn't we start earlier in the evening?"

"From the way you're beginning to sound, we started soon enough. Anyway, Carl became chef for the American generals after the Germans retreated from Paris. He became a favorite of the Allied supreme commander and was able to get into the United States shortly after the war ended. We moved to New York after Carl became assistant chef at the Waldorf Hotel. Mother was still determined to give me the best education and to shelter me from all men until she picked the right one for me."

"What did Carl say about this?"

"He couldn't say anything. He only worked hard and let mother rule both of us. I was an accelerated student in high school and college, which enabled me to finish my M.S. last year. I cut the strings to mother when I got the research job, and I've tried to have a great time since. She thinks I'm going to ruin my life, but she doesn't understand that the social life is different here from hers in France."

"Enough history. Let's finish the wine and drive back to Handover with the wind in your hair and your cares lost in the speed of the car."

"You poetic Southerner. I could kiss you over and over."

"Where have you been so long? Look at what I've missed—good wine, beautiful scenery, and kissing a gorgeous woman."

"The night has only begun, and if we survive the wine, it will be beautiful. But one never becomes immune to the effects of wine, the drink of the gods."

Roosevelt arrived with the check, and reality. One quick look and my eyes opened wide—$12.95 per bottle! Roosevelt whispered that he was able to get one bottle taken off the check and even returned my dollar tip.

"I know you guys aren't making much at Handover, so consider the wine a gift from a fellow Southerner. You may not make much money, but you sure know how to pick a great looking gal."

The drive down the dirt road to the expressway was much more difficult than in the other direction earlier. The white birches reflected the car lights and seemed to get closer with every curve. Yvonne was right, the wine had gotten to me. I hit the brakes too hard on the last sharp curve and slid off the road. I thought Yvonne would have been scared after that, but it was obvious that the wine had gotten to her too. She held her head against the window pane, as if to try to cool it.

We made the drive back in what must have been record time, with Yvonne holding her head against the window all the way.

The parking lot at the Mansion was jammed. I couldn't get the car in the circular drive where Monk had told me to leave it because the Carriage Room crowd had parked everywhere. It had been raining, and everyone tried to drive up from the Tally-Ho. The only place I could find was at the edge of the pine grove.

For my present purposes the parking spot was perfect. We definitely didn't need anything else to drink, so under those conditions, with a beautiful woman high on romance and wine, only one course of action remained. I pulled her close to me, gently stroked her hair out of her face, and softly kissed her eyes, nose, and lips.

"You are beautiful."

"Really?"

"The most beautiful woman I've ever known."

"Really?"

"I could kiss you for hours and hours."

"Oh."

"I could kiss you all over."

"Oh, that's interesting.

For someone who had been so romantic earlier, she just wasn't coming on as I had expected. She let me kiss her all I wanted, but without any response. Lips that had been sensuous earlier in the evening were now limp. I started kissing her neck and ear, touching her as gently as I knew how, hoping to get some reaction. The rain and my heavy breathing caused the car windows to fog up. Good enough—if I couldn't see out, then no one could see in. So I began undressing her.

Yvonne was like a mannequin. She didn't move a muscle. Not one "don't" or "please don't do that." I couldn't believe it was so easy; in fact, so easy that it wasn't exciting at all. My affectionate touching and kissing seemed to be wasted as I tried every scheme I knew to get her excited. I had read about guys having sex with dead women, or one who *acts* dead, but it wasn't for me. Finally she made a response:

"I'm sick, let me out."

She managed to get her head out of the door before throwing up, and continued to throw up. I tried to hold up her head and help her as much as I could, but her sickness soon became contagious. Up came my wine, right inside the car, and my first thought was how was I going to explain this mess to Monk and Mario.

I jumped out of the car and threw up again. Yvonne had passed out, sprawled on the front seat. Although I was concerned about leaving her, I had to get some water and a towel to clean her up and get her dressed. My tent was nearby, so I figured I could get there and back in five minutes with the towel and water. She was asleep and would be all right in the car if Mario didn't find her.

I ran through the pine grove to my tent and almost bashed my head against a limb. My face was badly scratched, but I didn't let the incident slow me down. The Carriage Room crowd was packed into the basement of the Mansion, overflowing to the staff dining room and the hallway to the showers. Several guys wised off about my face being scratched and delayed me in getting to the staff shower. Luckily, I found two paper cups for the water and wet the towel. I wasn't sure I could remember where the car was, but I pushed my way through the crowd and angered a guest I collided with. The rain was pouring down as I ran to the car, only to find that I was on the wrong side of the pine grove and had to cut through again. I managed to miss the limbs but was covered with mud when I slipped on the bank in the parking lot.

The car was easy to find because the door was open with the dome light on, but Yvonne was gone. What had been a romantic night, full of promising adventure, had become a nightmare. Where do you start looking for a drunk, nude woman who has passed out in the woods during a downpour? I didn't know what to do. Apparently she hadn't tried to get back to her room, since her clothes were still in the car.

I couldn't call her, because there were other couples in nearby cars. After circling the car several times and calling her in a whispered voice, I decided that she couldn't have gone very far. It was so dark that I couldn't see a damn thing anyway, so I got down on all fours in the mud and began to crawl around. I was right. She hadn't gone very far. She had crawled under the car and passed out again.

The rain had let up, and I was able to stand her up against the hood of the car and wipe the mud off her. She kept repeating, "I'm sorry, mama, I won't do it again."

All I could think of was getting her dressed and cleaning up the car before Mario found me. Getting her dressed was one big problem. I had some experience in taking off bras and panty girdles, but I had never put any on, especially someone as limp as Yvonne was. I finally put them in her purse and dressed her the best I could. We started toward the Mansion only to discover the biggest problem of all—she had no idea where her room was, or at least she couldn't tell me.

It took me several minutes to literally drag her across the pine grove to my tent, for to be seen in our condition would have meant my being fired. Soaking wet and muddy, I finally got her to the tent. Fortunately, no one else was there, so I undressed her again, put one of my flannel shirts on her, and pushed her up into my bunk. My plan was to sleep until 6:30 and slip her back to her room before anyone else woke up. I got out of my wet clothes and put on an old sweatshirt to keep warm, for the morning air was getting very cold.

My bed had been short and narrow for me alone, but now seemed cozier and more comfortable with her in my arms. She was beginning to regain consciousness as I pushed her hair from her face. She smiled and snuggled close. Just holding her was a good as having sex.

"You're wonderful," I whispered as we both fell sound asleep, warm and dry at last.

Chapter Seven

 Tennis and Square Dancing

R and was shaking me. "Claxton, wake up, it's 7:30. We've got to eat and meet Sara on the tennis court at 8 o'clock."

"I don't want to get up. Where's Yvonne?"

"You're dreaming. Get up!"

"Damn it, where's Yvonne?"

"Look, there's no Yvonne, so get up."

"Oh shit, I'm not dreaming. She was here." I sat up in bed, but a searing pain shot through my head. I lay back, rolled onto my stomach, and buried my head under the pillow. The edge of a small, stiff piece of paper struck me in the eye. I pulled it out to toss it to the floor when I noticed writing on it—large letters, written with a piece of lipstick and visible in the dim light. I made it out a word at a time: "Thanks for taking care of me. Y." I groaned and buried myself once again in the bedding.

"I can't make it, Rand."

"You're the one who got us this job, so get your ass ready. I'm not going back to work for Mike."

"All right, I'll get dressed, but I'm dying. You'll have to help me if I get sick."

The cold morning air revived me somewhat, but the smell of food in the staff dining hall made me yearn for the bed again.

"I can't eat anything."

"Oh yes you can. The best cure for a hangover is to get some food in you to absorb the booze."

"I'll throw up if I eat anything."

"That'll be good for you; then you can eat some more."

"Where in the hell did you get your medical training, at a slaughterhouse?"

"Eat your pancakes and sausage whether you like it or not. We're going to meet Sara on time, even if I have to drag you out there."

I tried hard to keep the food down, but as I finished my coffee my stomach was in my throat. I ran to the john and threw up everything I had eaten. This was bad enough, but I continued to have the dry heaves. All I wanted was to go back to the tent and crawl into my bunk.

Stanley and Max were shaving and getting ready to serve breakfast at 9 o'clock. I hadn't seen them when I rushed into the stall, but they were enjoying my misery.

"Hey Stanley, looks like Clax really hung one on last night."

"You know how these young kids are the first time away from home. They think they know how to hold their booze."

"Probably tried to out drink Gloria again."

"Naw, I think he tried to make Yvonne, that lush Fran has been screwing."

By accident or intent, one of them pushed the stall door into me just as I was giving a big heave. I fell forward and got the stuff all over my clothes.

"You bastards, I'll get you for that."

"Oh fuck you. You won't make it through the season. If you can't hold it down, don't drink."

I wanted to knock the shit out of them, but I certainly wasn't going to try that in my present condition.

"We should get a picture of him for Mario to show at the next staff meeting. 'Now guys, here's what happens to you if you booze too much.'"

"If he can't hold his booze any better than that, he won't *be* here for the next staff meeting."

"You bastards drop dead."

They left laughing. Shortly afterward I wobbled out and headed back to my bunk. This was definitely not going to be my day.

It's 8 o'clock, said Rand. "Get the hell out of that bunk and change clothes. Damn, you stink!"

"I can't get up. My head is coming off and my stomach is upset."

"I brought you some aspirin and cola from Tent One."

"Those bastards."

"Ease up. They don't like you either, but can sympathize with a bad hangover."

Sara was waiting for us on the back courts. She needed three courts prepared for her 10 o'clock lesson. Mario had made a big thing out of the free tennis lessons, and large groups were showing up.

"Good morning, fellas!" she said enthusiastically. I shivered.

"How much work do you have for us on the courts?" asked Rand. "I have to meet Mike at 10 o'clock to find out what to do about the pool."

"Mike's crew put some calcium chloride on the courts yesterday, which is keeping them damp, and the rain last night makes them easy to work. I want to water them a little, roll them, and go over them with a broom. That and sweeping the line shouldn't take over an hour."

"When will we do the others?"

"You can work on them after lunch or maybe start earlier tomorrow. For now, you get the roller from the front court, and I'll start wetting these so you can get started rolling them."

The roller seemed to weigh a ton, and we had to pull it up a terrace to the front courts. I wasn't much help at all, for once I got hot I had to get some water quickly or else start throwing up again. It took us almost an hour to roll the courts. We could have done it much quicker if I had helped pull the roller, but all I could do was lean on it. Rand let me know that I owed him one.

He pulled the broom over the courts while Sara and I swept the taped lines. Before we could put up the nets the students, all girls, began assembling. Sara let me finish the lines while she went to the Mansion to get the practice balls and racquets. I had to make a quick trip to the john or make a scene at the courts. My head was still pounding, but I had to make it through the day. Then Don Williams was on the loudspeaker announcing the activities of the day.

"Good morning, everyone, this is Don Williams, your social director. We have a full day planned for you, followed by a full evening of activities. At 10 o'clock on the back courts, Sara, our tennis pro, and her staff will give tennis lessons for both beginners and advanced players. For those of you who prefer golf, lessons will be given at 10 o'clock on the practice green. Fran will be your instructor."

"Lunch will be served by the pool for those of you who don't want to dress, and at 2 p.m. the water volleyball game will get underway. Tennis is scheduled for 2 o'clock for advanced players. At 3 o'clock the staff softball team will play the guest all-stars.

"We also have some exciting activities planned for this evening. Happy hour with the Stompers will begin at 5 o'clock, and dinner will be served at 6:00. At 8 o'clock the hayride will leave from the Mansion, and at 10:00 we'll have our first square dance in the Tally-Ho."

Sara had begun the lesson when I got back. She had taken the intermediate players on two of the courts and had given me the others on the third court.

"Ladies, this is my assistant, Claxton. He'll be teaching those of you who have never played before. I just heard he is suffering from a terrible hangover, so go easy on him."

I winced. Whoever told her about my misery will probably be bellowing about it on the public address system next. But my immediate problem was the crowd facing me—20 girls expecting me to teach them to play tennis! Where do I start? Why the hell didn't Sara give me some sort of guidance? Well, I had to open somehow:

"Good morning, ladies."

"Good morning, Claxton."

"Have any of you ever played before?"

A short, plump girl raised her hand. "My girlfriend and I tried to play yesterday, but we lost all the balls."

"Well, maybe I can show you how to hit straighter."

"Have you played much, Claxton?"

"Yes, on my high school and college tennis teams."

"Where did you go to college?"

"You've never heard of it—Coyee College in South Carolina."

And then from my aching, muddled head I came up with a motivational opening to the tennis lesson that immediately got their attention:

"How many of you like to dance?" Most of them raised their hand.

"Well, if you can dance you're well on your way to being a tennis player, because they both involve balance and movement. All you have to do is move to the ball and hit it over the net."

"That sounds easy, but it isn't. How do you get the ball to stay in the court?"

For one who grew up playing tennis in a tee shirt and jeans, I couldn't believe how fashionable and expensive looking their tennis outfits were. These girls, who couldn't play at all, were dressed in the latest styles. Not only that, but their racquets where of the newest designs, and also expensive. Their philosophy seemed to be, if you look good you should be able to play good.

"We have only four days of lessons, so we will work one day on each of the basic strokes. Let's start with the forehand." I assumed the classic forehand position: side toward the net, knees slightly bent, weight balanced, racquet behind and level with my waist.

"This is called the forehand because you hit it from the right side with the front of the racquet."

"What do you call it if you're left handed?"

"You also call it a forehand—I should have said *strong* side, not right side." I turned and faced the other direction. "Now, when you hit the ball with the back of your racquet, you call it the backhand. Who knows another stroke?"

"The drive?"

"No, that's in golf. You call the stroke that starts a tennis game a serve, and that's done by throwing the ball up in the air and hitting it—like—this. The last stroke we'll work on is called the volley, which is when you hit the ball before it bounces."

"Claxton, can you teach us all that by Friday? Mario told me that I would be ready to play games by this weekend."

"Well, I'll show you the strokes during the lessons, but you'll have to practice on your own every day to learn them."

I was beginning to see why Sara gave me the beginners. She had a larger group, almost 30 girls, but they were the ones who knew a little about tennis. As to the non-tennis attributes of my group, most were average looking but two of them were very attractive, with form-fitting outfits. One of those, a tall brunette, seemed to be sizing me up, including the crotch area. She wore a low-cut blouse to show off a well developed chest. I decided she would certainly make an excellent model for demonstrating tennis techniques.

"The grip is a very important part of your swing. Spread your hand out on the strings and slide it down the shaft until you get to the grip and wrap your hand around it. Why don't all of you try it. That's right, spread your fingers out on the strings."

"My hand is too small to wrap all the way around like yours."

I had worked my way toward the buxom brunette, making her appear to be convenient for demonstration purposes. I stood behind her and held her spread right hand on the strings.

"Now look, keep your knuckles on top of the shaft as you slide your hand down."

She was wearing a fantastic perfume, something like wild gardenia. I wanted to wrap my arms around her and kiss those gorgeous boobs. At the age of 20, I was rarely too sick to be horny.

"When you wrap your hand around the grip, be sure to spread your fingers so that your thumb will be between your index finger and your middle finger."

"You mean your social finger," she said, pushing back against me with her ass against my crotch. I blushed and all of the students laughed except for a late arrival—Yvonne.

"If you can't touch your index finger, then your grip is too large and you won't be able to control your racquet. Now, does everyone have the correct grip? You must hold the racquet correctly to hit the ball on the strings and not the frame.

While they practiced their grip I tried to make sure they did it correctly, but my attention had suddenly shifted to Yvonne, who was practicing with the experienced players on the next court. Sara had selected her to demonstrate certain strokes, and to my surprise Yvonne hit very well. My head was splitting, and I felt like I would throw up any minute, yet there was my drinking companion Yvonne running and hitting the ball like a tournament player. Could this possibly be the same girl who had slipped out of my tent this morning? Not only did she play well, but she looked great in her light blue terrycloth outfit.

"Okay, everyone, check the grip one more time before I show you how to hit the forehand. That's good. Now look, this is the ready position. You face the net, leaning forward. When your opponent hits the ball, you move to return it. If it's to your forehand, then you turn your body so that your shoulders will be perpendicular to the net, racquet back, and you hit the ball with a low to high stroke. Remember, good preparation means a good stroke."

"Do you turn on your front foot or back foot?" asked the brunette, with a radiant smile. What a doll! Inviting me to come on, and I can't do anything about it.

"What's your name, miss?"

"Ginger."

"Well, Ginger, why don't you demonstrate the forehand stroke while I assist you. Okay, get in the ready position."

"Tennis or other?" More laughter.

"Tennis for now. Good, move to the backstroke and stop. You see that the racquet is back parallel with the shoulders."

When she turned I thought her boobs would pop out of her blouse. They were fantastic and she was fully aware of my interest.

"If I took the racquet out of Ginger's hand now and told her to hit the ball with the palm of her hand, it would be the same idea as hitting it with the racquet. See, the racquet is only an extension of the hand. Now bring the racquet around, starting low and ending high."

I wanted to work with Ginger all morning, but I could see several girls in the back whispering and looking unhappy. So I stepped back and assumed an air of impartiality.

"Does everyone understand the ready position and backstroke?" I started demonstrating the stroke and showing how to follow through to the ready position. This required more activity than I had anticipated, and I immediately felt sick again.

"Okay, ladies, line up and practice moving from the ready position to the forehand stroke ten times each while I make a quick trip to the Mansion."

"Hurry back, don't fall in." Laughter.

I made it to the john just in time. I washed off my face with cold water and felt much better. Even the headache was improved. Rand's cure was successful after all—get food in you, and it will absorb the booze. I rushed back to the courts to find an unexpected visitor, the big boss himself.

"Claxton, the girls tell me you are doing a great job."

"Thank you, Mario, they are very pleasant to work with."

"Yes, Ginger said you were very helpful in correcting her grip and forehand."

"I think Ginger can become a very good player with a little more practice."

Mario went into his gaze-over-your-shoulder act again, and I sensed that something was on his mind that I wouldn't like.

Say, Claxton, several of the girls have asked that you and Sara play an exhibition match. A good time might be tomorrow during happy hour. Sara is agreeable, and I'm sure you are too, so I'll make the announcement."

"I probably won't play well on such short notice."

"But good enough for a show, and to let the guests know about the tennis program. There's been a good response so far, and I'd like to keep the interest high. Anyway, I'll see you at your exhibition. Good luck!"

That fink! Even if I rested all day I still wouldn't be ready to play with so little practice. I was feeling better, but still hadn't fully recovered.   The delectable Ginger approached.

"Oh Claxton, Mario said you and Sara are going to play an exhibition match tomorrow. I'll be there to check your strokes and see if you play as good as you teach." "Thank you, Ginger, but I'm afraid you may be disappointed."

"Oh, no. Mario told us that you were the Southern Collegiate Champion!" Not knowing how to respond to that fallacious bit of information, I resumed the lesson.

"Okay ladies, each of you get a ball out of the basket and stand facing the fence. I want you to take your racquet back, drop the ball with your left hand, and hit it against the fence. I'll try to help each of you, and you can leave when you get tired. Tomorrow we'll work on the backhand."

I didn't anticipate such a disaster. The balls went in every direction—over the fence, into other courts, and off the handles onto their bodies. I guess we were lucky that no one was hurt. These New York girls may be good dancers, but they totally lacked the hand-and-eye coordination needed for tennis.

"That's very good ladies, just keep swinging smoothly, not too hard. Be sure to get the racquet back, drop the ball with your left hand, and hit with a rising racquet. Also, stand well apart so that no one gets hit by a ball or by a racquet that slips from somebody's hand."

Sara had been working on serves, but this all came to a stop when balls hit by my people started bouncing all over her courts. Her students were kept busy dodging and returning them. Yvonne and the other advanced students seemed fascinated by the confusion the beginners had created. Finally Sara came over to me.

"That a great drill for the forehand, but could you hold it until I finish with the serve in my lesson? I'm afraid someone will step on a loose ball and get hurt."

"Okay, I'll work individually with them now." Sara left. "Let me have your attention ladies. I'm going to start working with you one at a time. I want you others to practice your swing while pretending to hit a ball."

My group reported a few problems:

"When I drop the ball to practice my swing, it won't bounce back high enough."

"My racquet is too heavy and tires my arm so much I can't swing."

I answered them in turn.

"Hold the ball higher to get a better bounce."

"As to tiring yourself swinging—that means you're making your arm do the work and not your whole body. Watch how I hit the ball—racquet back, be sure your grip is correct, drop the ball, and lean forward as you swing the racquet from low to high. Can anyone tell me why you hit up on the ball?"

"To lift it up over the net?"

"Right you are, Ginger. Now, who will demonstrate for us how it's done?"

For me, the next 30 minutes were sheer hell. Every girl was trying her best, but only rarely was a ball hit solidly. At the moment, going back to the ground crew seemed rather appealing.

Sara's group had finished and were leaving the court. I had hoped that Yvonne would wait until I finished with my group, but she left with the others. Was she mad at me about something?

"It's 11 o'clock girls, so why don't we stop for now so you can get ready for lunch? Try to practice some more, but don't overdo it. We'll work on the backhand tomorrow. Thank you all for coming."

"That Mario's some showman, isn't he?" asked Sara.

"He thinks he is, but what could I do about the match? He wanted it played, and if I refused I'd be on the next bus South. Well, anyway—was the lesson satisfactory?"

"No one will ever know but us. Mario thought we did a great job, so we were successful."

"I didn't realize that adults could know so little about tennis, but maybe I gave them a start."

"It doesn't really matter, because most of them will never play seriously anyway.

"What time do we start this afternoon?"

"Try to be here by 1:30 so we can sweep the lines and get ready for the 2 o'clock class. Right now, let's get some lunch."

Sara went on to her tent and I took the balls and racquets to the office. Since Yvonne had rushed off, I hoped that Ginger would stay around after we finished, but she also left with the others. This place seemed to go to extremes—either you were deluged with women or they all deserted you. I couldn't understand the situation. Ginger led me on with the big tease, while Yvonne played the iceberg. That damn Monk would have probably screwed both of them right on the court. Oh well, the season is still young.

I was able to eat early and get back to the tent for a little nap before Rand, J.T., and Monk came in. One thing is certain about lunchtime—there is no wasted conversation or intentional interruptions of naps. I didn't hear the others come into the tent, but they also had passed out. Just a short nap would have been great, but we were awakened by a familiar voice: "Okay you guys, let's get back to work. J.T. and Monk, I want you to help Rand get the pool set up for the show and then wash the cars. Claxton, Williams is looking for you." Fuck you Mike, I thought.

I managed to struggle out of bed and start toward the social director's office in the Mansion. What misery to be half awake and not know what's in store for you. Maybe he would fire me. At least then I could get back to sleep for the afternoon.

I stopped for a moment at the staff washroom, and splashing some cold water on my face cleared my head a little. As I passed the terrace dining room, several of the girls in my tennis group waved cheerfully. And then a distressing sight: seated at a corner table overlooking the pool was Yvonne, in a lovers' reunion with the Adonis of the resort staff, Fran.

Well damn her, I thought, last night she couldn't get away from him fast enough and today it's all open affection. If I live to be a hundred I'll never understand women. You try to be nice to them and you end up getting the shaft. Monk's right. Just ask them directly if they want to screw; and if not, move on to another.

Williams was waiting for me in his office. I had no idea what he wanted, but was certain it wouldn't be anything I liked.

"Hi, Claxton, I'm glad you could make it before the afternoon tennis lessons. Mario was very impressed with the morning session and is looking forward to your match with Sara at happy hour tomorrow. I think we'll have a good turnout. He's even planned to set up a bar on the terrace.

"Look, Don, I'm not good enough to play Sara or anyone else in a match. I'm way out of shape, and I just haven't played much since last summer."

"That doesn't matter. Just put on a show, do the best you can—don't worry about winning. Mario wants something that will stimulate interest in tennis. He's spent a lot of money putting in and maintaining those tennis courts, not to mention hiring a professional instructor, and people don't seem to be using them enough. Word gets around in this business, and if you have good facilities and interesting activities planned, you get more paying customers."

"Well, I'll do my best, but I just hope I don't get too embarrassed."

"And don't worry about playing against Sara. A man should be able to beat a woman, right?"

"Not if the woman's Doris Hart or anybody who had steady strokes."

"Well enough about that for now. There's something else I'd like to talk about. We have a problem with our staff square dance exhibition team. One member from last year that we were counting on didn't come back this year, and I'm in a bind to replace him. Since you now work on my staff, I want you to replace him."

"But I don't know anything about square dancing in sets. All the square dancing I've ever done has been a little at school."

"It's all the same. You do the same steps and just change partners by following the caller's directions."

"Don't you need to practice something like that before you put on an exhibition? I don't see how I could get much practice in with the tennis lessons at 2 o'clock, helping Rand with the pool, and trying to sharpen my tennis before tomorrow."

"That's no problem. You can skip the work on the pool and plan to meet Stanley and the team at the Tally-Ho at 3:30 for practice."

"Stanley! I can't stand that shitass! Vice versa too, I guess."

"Look, he knows what he's doing with the dance team. Actually, I'm not crazy about him either, but he's been here so long that I have to get along with him."

"Who else is on the team?"

"The men will be you, Stanley, Fran, and Max."

"Holy Jesus, those guys hate my guts and will put it to me any way they can. Don't you know about the truck incident, and so on?"

"Everybody knows about that, including Mario. He also knows who used his car without permission and smelled it up. So, my advice to you is to do as you are told or plan to go home early."

"Looks like I don't have much choice."

"That's right, but neither do I."

"Well, who are the girls in this thing?"

"The four girls from Virginia." The Virgins!

"Well, they'll make it interesting. They seem to be pretty well liked."

"Be there at 3:30 for practice, and please, Claxton, don't get into any more fights with the waiters."

To my relief, the afternoon tennis and square dance sessions went very well. I finished lunch early and was able to hit with one of the more experienced girls in the afternoon session for the more advanced tennis players. My timing was better, but I still moved too slowly for a match, even if it was with a woman.

Stanley had been a real takeover guy at the practice session and I had followed Don's advice to keep my mouth shut and follow directions. I hated to admit it, but Stanley did know what he was doing. In an hour's time we were dancing like pros. The gals were really sharp, for all of them had danced extensively at school in Virginia and in local theater companies. Like Don said, all you had to do was follow the caller's directions.

After dinner I got back to my tent about 8 o'clock and hoped to catch some sleep before the square dance exhibition that evening. Our demonstration wasn't until the hayride ended, about 10:00 or 10:30 p.m., which gave us time for one more quick rehearsal. Stanley had announced that the dancers would meet at 9 o'clock at Tent One for a drink or two to loosen everyone up. But here I was trying to get a little sleep beforehand, and not able to do anything but toss, turn, and worry. Stanley's show of friendship made me uneasy—after all, I was a couple of tricks up on him and he was due some revenge. I was sure they were up to something.

Monk and Rand had gone on the hayride and J.T. had driven a group to the Stockbridge theater, so I was alone in the tent, not only unable to sleep but also without anyone to share my thoughts. Rand and I had sat in on many long bull sessions at school, but in this new job I had no one to talk with. Sara seemed friendly, but for some reason I didn't want to trust her with my problems, especially since she reported directly to Mario.

As much as I disliked the Tent One group, I had to admit that they knew how to pour a good drink. Stanley was the perfect host, and as soon as I'd finish a drink he would fix me a fresh one. After three quick drinks I was beginning to think that these guys were okay once you got to know them.

The Virgins, as the group of four girls from Virginia actually called themselves, were pretty well zonked after the third drink. I had forgotten about the dance and almost everything else except the Virgins. Somehow I had never seen them at the pool, but in their Daisy Mae dance costumes they looked great.

Pat was a tall girl with shapely legs who danced with Stanley. Jane, Max's partner, was a short, cute blonde with nice boobs. The best looking of the Virgins, Kay, was Fran's partner. Kay had an angelic face, and was the most virginal looking of the Virginia group. My partner was Bonnie—not the prettiest but by far the best dancer. She was also new to the team, so we at least had that in common.

By 10 o'clock I was ready for anything except dancing. We floated to the Tally-Ho and went through a quick rehearsal without any problems. Bonnie kept me on my feet and led me through the steps all the way.

The hayriders returned about 10:30 and the dance was underway as soon as the band got set up. We were all sitting on the patio waiting for Mario to announce us. Everyone looked totally crocked, though I sensed that I was feeling the booze more than anyone else.

I remember leaning over to roll up my pants legs, and before I knew it I had let out a tremendous blast of air. Jane, who had been sitting next to me, jumped up, pointed to me with wild laughter, and yelled: "He pooted!" Amid the laughter, Bonnie said: "Oh no, Jane, that was a full-sized *fart*." At that moment, Mario arrived and greeted everyone in the room.

"Hi, gang."

"Hi, Mario."

"Everyone having a good time?"

"Yeah!"

"Well, we've got much in store for you. We want all of you to learn to square dance and have a great time. Now here is Stanley, our headwaiter, and our square dance exhibition team." I was pretty groggy when we made our entrance as rehearsed—a promenade with Stanley and Pat leading the way. He took the microphone.

"Hi everyone, I'm Stanley from Nashville, Tennessee, and my partner is Pat from Richmond, Virginia. Next is Max from Charlotte, North Carolina, and his partner Jane from Norfolk, Virginia. Then we have Fran from Montgomery, Alabama, and his partner Kay, from Charlottesville, Virginia; and last but not least, Claxton from Savannah, Georgia, and his partner Bonnie from Lynchburg, Virginia. We are going to demonstrate several basic movements and then put them together in dances you will be doing."

The caller took the microphone and explained the basic movements—bowing to the corner, now to your own, swing to your corner and now your own, and the promenade bit. So far I thought I was doing pretty well, but Bonnie kept punching me in the ribs, especially when I turned the wrong way or stepped on her foot. Now for the big test.

The caller announced the first dance as "Marching through Georgia." We had rehearsed this with a record and I thought I went through it okay, but Bonnie gave me several jabs to remind me of my mistakes. I did a bit better on the next dance, "Bird for the Cage," which we had also rehearsed. Then came a surprise. Stanley announced that we would now do something special. I had no idea what that would be, but when everyone applauded with anticipation I smiled in acknowledgment along with the rest of the team. I quickly lost the smile when Bonnie leaned over and asked, "What in the hell does he mean by 'special'? We didn't practice anything else."

"Maybe it's just an extension of the things we rehearsed," I said, trying to reassure myself as well as her.

"Surely he's not going to embarrass us in front of everyone."

"Not Stanley. Don told me that he knew what he was doing and that we could depend on him."

"Oh, bull."

I didn't hear him announce the name of the dance, but I did hear him say that he had a few surprises and everyone would like it. It started out fairly easy with the basic steps, but at a much faster tempo. Even as high as I was I began to realize that I had been sucked into a trap, and the frightening thing was that I couldn't do anything about it.

We circled rapidly to the right and then back to the left, and before I could get my balance Bonnie and I were in the middle of the circle with everyone flying around us. We wound up at the tail of a twisting, intertwining line. Just as the line was clearing the last twitching movement, Stanley led the line behind me and tripped me from the rear. I made a full turn and landed on the floor. The others kept dancing as I staggered up, but Max exacted a bit of revenge for my earlier "victories" over him by stepping on my fingers as he danced by.

Bonnie helped me up, and the crowd applauded wildly. They seemed to appreciate my "drunk" act. At this point, what he had put me through certainly should have been sufficient punishment for my past misdeeds, but Stanley wasn't satisfied. He continued the dance with steps that I couldn't do even if I were sober. Bonnie and I struggled to keep up, but we looked like two amateurs in a professional company.

When the thing finally ended, Stanley took the microphone to express his regrets that Claxton and Bonnie had such difficulty with the dance, explaining that they were new to the team and would improve with time. I could understand his revenge motive toward me, but only a real shitass would embarrass Bonnie as he did.

Bonnie and I had some compensation—we had won the sympathy of the crowd, as indicated by the applause for us when we left the stage. Mario approached.

"Say, Claxton, that was some show you put on. The guests loved it."

"Thanks, Mario."

I think you and Bonnie won the crowd by showing that anyone can make a mistake. It will make them more willing to try the square dancing."

"I'm glad it worked out that way."

"As a matter of fact, I'll make sure Stanley keeps that routine in his show for that purpose. You're a great showman . . . you know how to win a crowd."

I could never figure Mario. He could have reprimanded me for being drunk and fouling up the dance, or Stanley for embarrassing a guest. But his reaction was that I'm a great showman. Won't this burn Stanley's ass after going to all the trouble of slugging my drinks to make me look ridiculous.

I got away from the Tally-Ho as quickly as I could. I was exhausted from last night, an eternity ago with Yvonne, and this day had seemed to drag on forever. Stanley's booze had made me a "great showman," but I needed to get into bed before my luck ran out.

Rand was in the tent waiting for Janet to return from the stables. He said they were going out, but I suspected he had planned an evening in the tent. Janet returned before I could give all the details, and I knew they had more interesting things to do. They left almost immediately with blanket and pillow for what they called star-gazing from the pine grove.

I crawled into bed exhausted, but very happy with myself over the events of the evening. By luck and a weird crowd of drunks, I had gotten the best of the waiters again, but here I was, alone. This wasn't what Handover was supposed to be about. What was I doing wrong? Rand had Janet, Monk could always score, J.T. would probably find something while driving, and I play games with waiters. Well, starting tomorrow I'm going to change all that. I'm going to find Yvonne and take up where we left off; and if not her, I'll try to make it with Ginger, or someone. Maybe Ann would come back and we could start over. But for now, sleep, wonderful sleep. For the first time since I had been at Handover, I slept like a log.

Chapter Eight

 Becoming a Boozer

Rand and J.T. had turned in late, but Monk still wasn't in when we went to breakfast.

"That damn Monk probably found someone to sleep with."

"The lucky shit has the morning off, too. I'd probably have to go to work at dawn if I lucked up."

"Don't worry, J.T., your chance will come."

"I thought I was about to score last night, but it's the same old story. They all back out when you get down to it. Can you believe I had this girl completely undressed in Mike's car, but she got scared and started crying. I couldn't do anything after that."

We finished breakfast and went back to the tent to collect the dirty linen and towels. Mario had posted a notice in the staff dining room that linens must be changed weekly. To our surprise, Monk, the great lover, was back in the tent sound asleep. We weren't about to let his story go untold; and anyway, he had to change his filthy linen.

"Monk, get your ass out of the bunk and take off the sheets. They have to be changed today."

"Oh, go to hell."

"Damn it, Mario said if you didn't change them today, you would be seeing him."

"I'll do it later."

"Hay, Monk, tell us where you were last night."

"To hell with you."

"Were you on the lawn with Gloria again?"

"Look, you pussy-starved bastards, it doesn't matter where I was."

"Hey, we got his temper up."

"It must have been Gloria again. The clap has reached his brain."

"You know, I could tell you guys any story I liked, and you would believe me. You'd really like to hear more Gloria shit, but I'm going to tell you the truth, and I bet you won't believe it."

"Monk, you *couldn't* tell the truth."

"The trouble with you guys is that you don't know what to do. I tried to tell you all you have to do is ask, and if you ask the right one, you score."

J.T. pondered that a moment.

"I've tried that, but no luck yet."

"J.T., you give up too easily. Keep asking and you'll find the right one."

"Well, anyway, what happened last night?"

"Do you remember the couple who played in the string band?"

"Yeah, the woman with the guitar and the man with the fiddle. Which one did you fuck?"

"Wise ass. Anyway, after the dance they all went back to the piano for some singing and serious drinking. The gal I was with got pissed off at me for something and left, so I joined the singing. The more I drank the better the guitar player looked."

"But what about her husband?"

"He was drinking that bourbon like it was water and got completely crocked. Pretty soon he passed out, but we kept on singing and drinking. First we played hands and knees, and before I realized it she was all over me. We finally broke off the singing, and I helped her get him to the car. She wanted me to drive them home and then drive her car back here where they would pick it up tomorrow."

"Then what?"

"Well, he passed out in the back seat. I started driving, and she really started loving me up. I said, whoa, won't he wake up? And she said no, when he passes out like that he is really out."

"Did you make out?"

"Don't rush me, I'm getting to that. We got to their house and drug him to the bedroom. I waited in the living room while she undressed him and made sure he was asleep. She came out in about ten minutes wearing only a black negligee."

"You really expect us to believe that shit?"

"You haven't heard the best part yet. She started laying it on, and suddenly there we were on the floor, her pulling off my shirt and me my pants. We were rolling back and forth, and then I got it out and was ready to put it in her when I looked up, and there was that damn husband of hers standing over me with a baseball bat!"

"Are you telling the truth?"

"So help me; I was scared to death. I grabbed my clothes and ran, and every time the drunk bastard would stumble and fall I'd stop and put something on. I was in front of his house buttoning the last button when they started yelling at each other. Then I heard him say that he was going to run me down. I assumed he meant with his car, so that sure as hell eliminated me hitchhiking back. I wasn't going to flag down any car with him on the road."

"How in the world did you get back?"

"Believe it or not, that's the best part of the story."

"C'mon, Monk, it couldn't get any wilder."

"I ran down the street for about two blocks and turned down some railroad tracks. They led me to a rail yard where a freight train was slowly passing through. It was headed toward Lenox and moving slow enough for me to get on. I was really lucky to find a way out of town. The train picked up speed, and I held on for dear life. Suddenly I realized the train was not heading south toward Lenox, but west toward Albany. By now it was moving too fast for me to jump off. You can't believe how cold it was! Finally, after an hour or so it began to slow down and enter another rail yard. I was able to jump off and thaw out."

"How did you get back to Handover?"

"The bus! I jumped off near Albany, and walked a mile or so until I found a Greyhound bus depot. So I caught a 6 a.m. bus to Pittsfield and hitchhiked to Handover. So here I am, safe, sound, and much wiser. I've learned not to fuck with a female guitarist whose husband plays in the same band."

"Great story, Monk! You're lucky to be here without a bashed noggin."

A minute or two later came a familiar call through the door of the tent:

"All right you guys, we've got work to do, so let's get to it."

That grating voice of Mike's—how good it was not to report to him. Rand and J.T. had to clean the pool before the guests arrived, which meant that I would have to do the courts by myself.

I arrived at the tennis courts to find Sara standoffish and unpleasant. She returned my greeting with a mumble, and in general had little to say. She let me off with just sweeping the courts and marking off the tapes (no rolling, thank goodness). I couldn't understand why she was so unfriendly unless she had a case of stage fright about the match, and was trying to hide it.

The teaching session wasn't as confusing as the first day, but I'd never seen a worse collection of backhands. Ginger wore an outfit even more revealing than yesterday's. As for the "other woman" in this situation, I tried to talk to Yvonne over with the experienced players, but she too was aloof and left right after the lesson ended.

Don had given the exhibition top billing over the public address system. You would have thought that Doris Hart and Jack Kramer were playing, and I really caught a lot of flack at lunch.

"And here is our star as he leaves the center court at Forrest Hills," I heard as I entered the staff dining room and sat next to Rand.

"Claxton, did you know that the waiters are getting a pool on the match? The odds are 3 to 1 in favor of Sara."

"I can't believe all this stuff, Rand. What difference does it make who wins?"

"They seem to think that it will embarrass you to be the underdog."

"They can think whatever they like. Right now all I want is to finish lunch and grab a nap."

Don made the announcement about the match again after lunch and really laid it on. He awarded me titles of Savannah City Champion, Georgia State Champion, and Southern Collegiate Champion.

A swim show ran from 2 o'clock until 3:30. Mario had set up the bar to serve both the swim show and tennis exhibition, selling drinks at half price to ensure a big crowd.

By the time Sara and I came onto the court the crowd was huge. Mario wasn't making much money on the discounted drinks, but was sure making a lot of guests happy.

We had a brief warm-up session, and Mario was about ready to plug the tennis program again. And then out came several leaping and yelling cheerleaders! I recognized them as staff girls who lived in Sara's tent, and they made their loyalty immediately apparent:

"Hit Clax high/Hit Clax low/Come on Sara/Let's see you go!"

The crowd applauded, and as I was trying to figure out the meaning of all this, up walked Mario.

"Hi, gang."

"Hi, Mario."

"Everybody having a good time?"

"Yeah."

"How was the water show?"

"Great!"

"Ready to watch some good tennis?"

"Yeaaaaaaah!"

"Don Williams has put together a good program in tennis, and I've made sure that we have the best facilities around." (Applause.) "We have a couple of champions here to play for you today, and I'll let Don tell you all about it."

"Thank you, Mario. This is like being at the Forrest Hills center court, except we're having a lot more fun, right?"

"Right!"

Williams went through all the bull about how good I was and how many titles I held, including the Southern Collegiate Championship. As far as I knew, there was no such title, and if there was I sure as hell had no claim to it. His introduction of Sara had her just a notch below Doris

Hart and brought down the house. Since most of the guests were women, I guess it was a natural thing, but the cheerleaders seemed to take it a little too far with:

"Clax is all done/He's had too many/After the match/Even one and he's done/Go Sara!"

What I couldn't understand was how and why I had been cast as the villain. Somehow this whole damn thing was planned, and Sara must be in on it.

Williams told me the match would be only one set, but was now announcing to the crowd that it would be the best two out of three. I didn't believe I could last that long, and I'm sure the crowd couldn't. Well, only one course remained open—if made into a villain, then play like one. Show no mercy to this female opponent, play her like a man.

Sara won choice of serve and went all out to take the first game. She hit deep to my backhand then came to the net for the put-away. I tried to pass her, but my backhand was too rusty for that. She won the first game easily, losing only one point on a missed volley. The crowd applauded wildly as we changed courts, and the cheerleaders were at it again:

"See Sara go/She's our champ/Clax is dumped/he's our chump/Yeaaaaah SARA!"   .

She stared right past me as we changed courts, and I saw that she was grim-faced and dead serious about winning the match.

I certainly never anticipated such a large crowd. They filled all three levels of the terrace leading to the courts and were standing on the lawn. The rush to the bar between games was a better show than the match. One of the ugly girls from the tennis class, out-and-out drunk, shouted from the terrace, "Where's your great backhand, Claxton?" That remark caused me to lose my temper, and without thinking I shouted back, "Oh, fuck you!"

She jumped up and yelled, "I'd love it!" This brought prolonged cheers from the crowd, which rattled me even more. I double faulted on my first serve, and the crowd cheered again. Was anyone out there pulling for me? But then my ensuing serves were pretty strong, forcing Sara into weak returns, and I won the game.

In the third game, I got going with good service returns and really hit well. I began to stroke the ball hard and deep, but Sara got everything back. We both played sound tennis for the next few games, and the crowd acted almost sober, enjoying the good play. At 4-all we had played several long games, and as I had expected I was getting tired. At 5-all I was exhausted, and she easily put away the set at 7-5.

The match should have ended there. One set would have been enough for that heavily boozing crowd, and they were beginning to lose interest in the match. I'm sure Sara recognized that I was exhausted, and might have at least let up a bit or acted more friendly. But she remained grim-faced and determined.

As I took the court for the second set, my mind was completely blown as I saw Yvonne leaving with Fran. I wanted to quit and just get out of this damn place. I had reached the point of not believing in anyone or about anything. How could Yvonne be acting like this, when we were so close just two nights ago?

Then Sara was serving. I got the ball back and waited for her to hit a deep return, but she had a new plan. Her drop shot barely cleared the net—not an outright winner, and one I could reach if I ran hard enough. I puffed my way to it but returned a weak shot. As I stood at the net, she lobbed the ball over my head for a winner. So the pattern was set for the second set. She was playing me the way I told her I had worn out my opponent for the junior championship in Savannah—running him to exhaustion in the heat.

Her strategy was good, but the resulting tennis was dull. Most of the crowd had gone by the time she ran up a 4-1 lead, and she wound up winning 6-2. We approached the net for the traditional congratulatory handshake.

"You played very well," I said.

"Thank you. I'm sorry you were so out of shape, but you played well too before you pooped out."

"I thought we were friends. I didn't expect you to go for the kill that way."

"We *are* friends, but I was pressured by Mario to try to make you look bad so that the girls would take more interest in the program. He wanted to make the guests believe that a woman would play well enough to beat a man—even a college athlete."

"Then I was the fall guy."

"Right, but it's over now; we've both done our job. Let's forget that and go to my tent and have that drink you passed up last week."

I had never before had alcohol either before or after competing in an athletic event, but I wasn't now at Coyee College and felt the need for something relaxing. I didn't know what effect the booze would have, but I was soon to find out. Sara and I were both too tired to eat dinner, so we consoled ourselves in drinks and a real gut conversation about Handover. She was unhappy with Mario and his showman tactics, but she couldn't quit because she needed the money. Her teaching job paid an income only ten months of the year, and a new car and furniture had her in debt.

I soon learned that a tired body and booze don't mix too well. I could hear her talking, but I couldn't put it together. She wanted to tell me about her problems and I wanted to figure out what the hell was going on with Yvonne and the others. After listening to her problems about her mother, boyfriend, and dog, I couldn't stand it anymore. Finally I blurted out, "Sara, I've been here six weeks without scoring. What am I doing wrong?" For a moment, she just sat there smiling. It occurred to me that she thought I wanted her, and was thinking of a nice way to say no.

"You know, Claxton, nothing would please me more than to make you happy, especially after this afternoon, but I've made a commitment that I have to live with. I'm older than most of the girls on the staff, so I don't have time to play the field. I have someone back home waiting for me, and although he may not be everything I desire, he wants me."

"That's not what I meant."

"I know what you meant, and I can help you."

"Please do."

"A man may think he knows when someone is available, but a woman knows another woman's feelings much better."

"That's good to know, but what am I doing wrong?"

"Let's take the case of Yvonne."

"To hell with her, she ran back to Fran."

"That's where you're wrong. She is still very interested in you, but she's too reserved to let you know until you make a move."

"I can't get close to her. She's with him every time I see her."

"You've got to let her know you care for her and give her the opportunity to make a move. She'll come to you if you let her, because she really likes you. Taking care of her when she was drunk rather than taking advantage of her was something she liked."

"How did you know about that?"

"Word gets around, and she knew you were not in shape to play on Tuesday. She didn't tell all, I'm sure, but enough. Let's have one more drink and call it quits."

"One more and I'm through for the week."

She rambled on about what a girl likes and dislikes, what to do and what not to do. After a while I couldn't understand what she was saying, but it was something about being gentle, kissing softly, being warm—the tender touch—and remember that the tease leads to success quicker than a confrontation. Our discussion was ended by the return of her tentmates. They were a bit embarrassed to see me, because of their "Hit Clax high/Hit Clax low" yells, and I was a bit annoyed to see them, so after a mumbled exchange of greetings and a quick goodbye to Sara, I took my leave.

As I passed Tent One, their party was in full swing. They saw me—in fact, I think they were on the lookout for me—and everybody yelled out a well rehearsed:

"Clax is all done/He's had too many/The match is over/He ain't worth a penny. YEAAAAAAAAA."

Fran was leading the yell, his arm draped around Yvonne. And Sara had said Yvonne was still interested in me! Well, he can have her, for now I'll take my bunk.

J.T. and Monk were driving guests to the theater again and were gone for the night. Rand and Janet were leaving the tent as I arrived. They had found a place out on the golf course that was great for star gazing, so with blanket in hand they left for an evening of "study." That guy always played it smart; even at school he had someone. He once told about this girl from Cuba who attended a private school in his home town while he was in high school. The love story ended, though, when he went home with her. She was from a wealthy political family who had sent her to the United States to be educated, not to find a husband. Rand was told that she would marry the person of their choice, and that a poor boy from south Georgia was not what they had in mind.

All this past year he had been involved with an exchange student named Hilda from Sweden. Some of us thought that they were sort of an odd couple because she had great difficulty speaking English. But she also was interested in the stars, and Rand always had a star-gazing blanket, and that apparently was all the communication they needed.

Sometime during the night, J.T. and Monk returned with two girls and tried to get me to drink with them. They were out of their minds and gave up when they couldn't get me awake even after sitting me up and pouring a drink down me. I did remain half awake. What a strange sensation that was—I could hear them laughing and talking, but couldn't fully understand what they were saying.

"Does he mumble like that all the time?"

"Naw, just when he's horny."

"Do you think he's all right, Monk?"

"Yeah, all he needs is a hot woman."

"How about two hot women?"

Then they were all standing next to me as I lay in a stupor in the top bunk. Monk was giving directions:

"Get those tennis clothes off; the pants too, Gloria."

"What in the hell is *this*?"

"You don't recognize that? It's called a jock strap."

"No wonder he can't get it up."

"Give him a good french kiss, Sue."

This had to be a dream, but I could see two blurred figures with long hair.

"Get it up, Gloria."

"I can't. This son of a bitch must be dead."

"Well, bless him with holy water and let's go."

"Don't waste the booze, Monk."

"To hell with the booze. Don't waste the women."

What happened after the blessing was beyond me, for I only remember being freezing cold and unable to pull up my blanket. They had left on the bright light in the center of the tent, which tortured my eyes. I was too drunk and sleepy to do anything about it.

After what seemed like hours of agony, things suddenly changed. Now I was warm, the room was dark, and I was being kissed by soft lips and touched by gentle, loving hands. I didn't dare open my eyes. If it was a dream, I didn't want it to end.

"Can you ever forgive me for being so unkind and unappreciative? You were so thoughtful, so generous to me when I needed you, and since then I've only hurt you. I don't know much about making love, but I want to make love with you anyway, and I can make you happy. I have to leave tomorrow, but I want this night to be one I will remember always.

"Please wake up. Please know what I feel for you; for after tomorrow I'll never see you again, but tonight will live forever."

But I couldn't wake up, until the next morning. On my pillow was a note written in red lipstick. "Thank you for letting me take care of you. Y."

Chapter Nine

❀ *Goodbye to Rand*

July seemed to fly by fast. Each week, the girls seemed to get better looking and the drinking crowds wilder. And at times it appeared that staff members were the wildest revelers of all.

Mario had really gotten upset over the drunken behavior of some of the staff members. Although he had never sent anyone home, he came close after J.T.'s and Monk's latest episode. On the night that I passed out in the tent, J.T., Monk, and the girls continued to party late into the night. No one objected to their partying, but they did cause a little disturbance when they went swimming in the buff.

Monk insisted they turn on the pool lights so no one would get hurt. So J.T., Monk, Gloria, and Sue put on a great show for the crowd on the terrace. Monk even gave a diving exhibition. He had been a good diver in high school and was in fine form that evening.

For safety reasons, a swimming pool at a resort would have only a low diving board or none at all. But with a view toward competitive diving shows, Mario had put in a high board with tremendous spring. Monk used all of that spring when he did a full gainer with double twist. His dive was well executed and brought applause from the terrace, but there was only eight feet of water under where he hit the surface. He crashed to the bottom of the pool, crushing a couple of vertebrae. Only the quick thinking of the people on the terrace saved him from drowning.

Mario paid the hospital bill and sent Monk back to South Carolina. It was later learned that he wasn't so much a wonderful guy as he was concerned that Monk's family would sue him for having such a strong board over only eight feet of water.

Mario, the promoter, was up to his old tricks again. He wanted a staff softball game between his team, which was composed mostly of waiters, and the other staff members, mostly ground crew. He felt that they were not getting any competition from guest teams and that the guests would prefer to watch and drink. Mike was directed to get the team in shape, which meant that we had one practice to get ready to play.

We should have realized after the practice that we were sitting ducks, since J.T., Rand and I were the only ones who knew how to catch the ball. The other guys from the ground crew and kitchen were helpless in the field. I thought that with J.T. on first, Rand at short, and me pitching we could get them out, but I was wrong. They had played enough to hit the low-pitched ball to the outfield, past our only good fielders. We didn't have anyone out there who could catch anything, so they began scoring a lot of runs.

Mario gave the game a big promotion and had the bar set up with drinks at half price again. He even put out a tub of beer for each team, which was our undoing. The game was called after five innings because some of the ground crew team was unable to find their positions on the field, with the score something like 31-2 in favor of the waiters.

There were always staff problems as the season entered August. Some people grew homesick, others caught prolonged colds, and some left because of personal problems. Sara departed because she was afraid she would lose her boyfriend back home, so I had the entire tennis program. She did tell me on departing that she just couldn't take Mario's unrealistic teaching conditions any longer . . . both the number of students and Mario's expectations of how much they could be taught.

The biggest shock came when Rand came in late one night and started making preparations to go home. Although we were friends, I had no inkling of any sort of major problems that would make him suddenly want to up and leave. Rand had been with Janet every night since the second week of June. I thought this was just his style—to go with only one girl rather than play the field as J.T. and I were doing. He seemed to have the situation with Janet under control until one day the unexpected happened; her former boyfriend returned.

Janet's boyfriend had joined the Navy in May and had gone away to boot camp. Everyone locally knew that they had been close but thought she had gotten over him when Rand came along. After boot camp he had a week's leave before going to sea, and came to Handover to try to win Janet back.

He didn't have enough money to be a guest, so he asked Mario for a job. Mario was a patriotic soul and wouldn't turn a sailor away if he could earn his keep, so Eddie was put on the ground crew. I saw him once or twice in the dining room but had no idea who he was, and Rand certainly made no mention of him. As far as I knew, things between Janet and Rand were the same; they continued spending a lot of time every night on the golf course or in the pine grove.

Since Yvonne, I had carefully avoided any involvements other than the direct method of let's drink and go at it. On the night of Rand's departure I had almost scored with two sisters from Hartford. We had gone to Blandtyre for drinks and my introduction to margaritas. The ride back was fantastic, and we ended up parking outside their cottage. I couldn't do much with two of them, so I selected the better looking one to zero in on. The other one got angry and left, so I thought the situation was working out fine. She was a great kisser, but when things reached the undressing stage she came up with a reason I hadn't heard before for keeping her panties on. She said she was married to a man who had a vasectomy, and if she became pregnant he would know she had been unfaithful!

Rand was already in his tent, packing his bags. He usually stayed out very late, so to find him in early was unexpected. At first he wouldn't talk, but there had to be some explanation. If he had problems at home, or a run-in with Mario, I wanted to help if I could. One good thing about a small school such as Coyee College was that one got to know people closely and could count on them when needed.

"Damn it, Rand, if you're packing you've got to be going somewhere.

"It doesn't matter where I'm going."

"What do you mean by that?"

"You know, if I want to go home I'll go, and I don't have to tell you why."

"If something's wrong at home, I want to help you. We've been friends too long. I can't just let you walk out on us."

"I appreciate that, but no one can help. There's nothing you or J.T. can do. I got myself into this mess, and I'll get out of it."

"You, J.T., and I came together, and we'll leave together. What do you mean, 'mess'?"

"Come on, don't make me go into it. Too many people are involved already."

"You've got to tell me. I'm leaving with you if you don't."

"It hurts too much, but I'll tell you what hurt is and hope you never go through it."

"It can't be that bad."

"Have you met Eddie, the guy who has been painting the front fence?"

"I've only seen him in the dining room."

"Well, he's Janet's old boyfriend, and is on leave from the Navy. He's here this week to try to win her back before he goes to sea."

"Can't you just wait him out and take over again when he's gone?"

"It doesn't work that like."

"Sure it does. There are plenty of girls here who would go wild over you. Remember Frances and the peek-a-boo shower? You could have slept with her all week."

"That's not my style. I like to hold onto someone, to be with them again and again. You saw that at school."

"Yes, you scored while most of us ran around in circles."

"Anybody can score—even Monk, but not many people find someone like Janet."

"Come on, she's not *that* great."

"Oh yes, I know you didn't like the smell of horses about her at lunch, but to me she was like the most beautiful flower ever grown."

"You really care for her."

"Damn right."

"Why don't you do something about it?"

"I can't. It's out of my hands."

"Bullshit."

"Do you know what her boyfriend did today?"

"Painted the picket fence, I suppose."

"Right, but did you know that ever so often he climbed the fence to paint the other side?"

"He's crazy. That fence is six feet high with sharp points."

"Right. Probably he was just trying to save time, not walking back to the gate. But the worst finally happened—he slipped and caught his leg on one of the points."

"Good God, that could split his leg open."

"It did. What's craziest of all is that he went back to his tent and didn't tell anyone. He was probably afraid he would lose his job. Mike found him late this afternoon and rushed him to the hospital before he bled to death."

"Dumb bastard," I said.

"That's just the beginning of the problem."

"Don't tell me that Janet ran to his bedside and dumped you."

"Perhaps not in that order, but with the same ending."

"Janet went to the doctor today and he confirmed that she's two months pregnant. I guess she had planned to tell me later, but his accident and near death changed the picture drastically."

"Come on, you're smarter than that. You wouldn't get her pregnant. Not a biology major."

"I didn't, but Eddie did. He came here to win her back but was crushed to learn that she wanted me. His injury wasn't part of his plan to get her back, but it almost ended his life."

"What did she do when she learned he was hurt?"

"She was totally confused at first, but when she learned how serious he was hurt, she ran to him thinking he had tried to kill himself over her. I waited for her to come from him hoping that we would remain the same and that he would go back to the Navy. She was crying, so we walked over to the park across from the hospital, and under the most beautiful moon you ever saw, she told me she loved him and would have his baby."

"How could she do you like that?"

"I guess I was an escape for her . . . until she had to face reality."

"She's still at the hospital and plans to stay there all night. I really feel sorry for her. She was wonderful."

"I think you really loved her."

"Oh yes, and still do. That's why I'm leaving."

"Come on, you haven't got to leave. We'll have some good parties, and you'll get over her. She's happy now. She's got what she wants."

"No, no. She wanted me. Things just happened. If I stayed and had to see her every day, I would go crazy. You can't stop loving someone in one day. What's worse is that I couldn't keep away from her, and I know we would be doing things that would hurt her even more. I don't think she could stand the pressure, so I guess I'm leaving because I love her enough not to complicate her life anymore."

J.T. came in a little later and also tried to get Rand to change his mind, but to no avail. So after a sleepless night, we drove Rand to the bus station where we tried again to get him to stay. When he got on the bus, we agreed that it didn't matter that much that he was leaving, since we'd be seeing him back at Coyee College in about a month. But we never saw Rand again. He joined the Marines and was in Korea when we last heard from him. His mother later wrote us that he was killed in action somewhere on the Chinese border when the Marines invaded North Korea and were overrun by the Chinese.

Chapter Ten

 Tanglewood and Jean

The low I felt over Rand's departure didn't last long. The week after he left proved to be one of the most exciting of my life.

My weekend duties were limited to keeping the courts up and scheduling court time, without any teaching responsibilities. This was about the only time I ever got to play, but after teaching and partying all week I usually had little enthusiasm for tennis on weekends. On Saturday morning, after I finished sweeping the lines, I had one of the most refreshing tennis experiences of the summer. Two sisters, Jean and Carm Vance from Boston, were hitting on the hard-surface court adjacent to the swimming pool. Their strokes and movement were beautiful to see. Finally, after hours of frustration working with girls who couldn't even get into the ready position, here were two girls with perfect form. Not only did their tennis look good, but they appeared to have just stepped from the pages of a fashion magazine. While I was plotting my approach to meeting one or both of them, Carm tripped and hurt her ankle. I rushed over to help her, and took advantage of the opportunity to introduce myself and congratulate them on their game.

"Have you been to Handover before?"

"We've been here for the last two summers. I don't remember seeing you."

"This is my first year here. I'm Claxton Carter, the tennis instructor."

"I'm afraid my tennis is over for a few days, Jean."

"Come on, Carm, we'll just get some ice on your ankle, and you'll be ready to play this afternoon."

"I don't think so. Maybe Claxton can sub for me."

My heart leaped at that prospect, but I effected modesty.

"Sounds great, but Jean appears to be too strong for me."

"Listen to him—just like all those other sweet talking Southerners. Don't trust him, Jean, I'll bet he's a heartbreaker."

"Oh Carm, don't be so hard on him. You know all Southern men are bashful and shy."

I helped them back to the Mansion, and Williams took over the care of Carm with a big fanfare. He was one of those people who made a big production of anything if he could get some attention from either the guests or Mario. Jean and I made plans to play tennis again at 3 o'clock that afternoon, over on the clay courts.

Also scheduled for 3 o'clock was a softball game that Williams set up between the staff team and a local softball team. Mario had never before let the local guys in except those who bought memberships (a select group—politicians and other people who could do Mario favors). Economic considerations aside, Mario was a snob. He regarded the local population as descendants of the people who were servants of the millionaires who had developed the area. Anyway, with the bargain drinks and the promotion given the softball game, the tennis courts were deserted except for Jean and me.

Never before or since have I enjoyed an afternoon of tennis like this one, on a cool and sunny day on a beautiful clay court surrounded by spruce and white pine trees. I liked the seclusion of the clay courts; they were away from the pool noise and non-tennis spectators. Jean played tennis with textbook precision. She was ready for every shot before the ball hit the court and returned the ball high over the net and always deep. The clay court gave a high, slow bounce, so I could get to all her shots. Under these conditions, and because I had learned to play tennis on red clay courts in Georgia, I was at my best.

We warmed up slowly, then hit corner to corner, first forehand then backhand. A half hour went by quickly, and it was I who needed to rest. Apparently Jean could have continued indefinitely.

"Your game is beautiful," I said. "You've had some excellent instruction to play so well."

"Carm and I took lessons at the public tennis center in Boston. You play well, too, especially your forehand. How did you learn?"

"I had a high school coach who helped me, but I always played with older players, and they made me hit out rather than punch the ball."

"They did a great job. You should be playing college tennis somewhere."

"I would like to play at school, but we only have occasional matches. Baseball is the only spring sport they emphasize."

"You could play on the teams in my area."

"Come on. I couldn't stay with those guys. Most of them have played the junior circuit and national tournaments. All I've played were high school tournaments."

"I've played with some of them, and I know you're at their level. Sure, the guys at the Ivy League schools are usually ranked pretty high, but there are many small schools who could use a player like you."

Motivated by those words of praise, I forgot my tiredness and we hit for another hour. She had me believing I was good, and in fact I had never stroked the ball better. I got set early, hit the ball in front of my body, and followed through smoothly. Hitting with Sara had been competitive, but Jean made me look and feel good. She never mentioned playing a set or any competitive drills, only good strokes and good positioning.

By 4:30 I had enough and was ready for the shower and the bunk. I was really flying high, but was uncertain what to do with Jean.

"Would you like to go to my tent for a drink?" I asked.

"I'd rather to go the library, have a Coke, and listen to the music that will be played at Tanglewood tonight."

"Are you telling me that I've found a Yankee lady who doesn't drink?"

"Nor smoke."

"Unbelievable."

"Not really. I believe that you can enjoy Handover much more without drinking. Why come on vacation to get drunk and feel terrible? I've seen enough drunks on my other trips here to last a lifetime, and it's not for me."

"I'm convinced. I'll have a Coke."

"Have you been to Tanglewood this summer?"

"No, I haven't."

"How about the dance festival or theater?"

"No, I've stayed on campus."

"You've missed the best part of the Berkshires. There's more here than you could see all year. We'll begin your education now with an introduction to Tchaikovsky."

The library was an area of Handover that I had not frequently visited. Surprisingly, since the library was not a revenue producer, Mario had made it into a beautiful room. His book collection included many volumes of Southern history, especially the Civil War period. Many stories about his interest in the war were told. He had spent days at Andersonville, Georgia, after reading Kapel's book. I never finished the book because I got nauseated reading about the horrible conditions at the Confederate prisoner-of-war camp.

The collection also included many books on Roman history and the Italian Renaissance, but unknown to me until now it also included an extensive collection of classical music. Of all the rooms in the Mansion, only this one reflected the taste and lifestyle of the original owners. The Steinway grand piano would have been out of place anywhere at Handover except in this room.

"Do you like Tchaikovsky?"

"Yes, what I know of him."

"Well, what is that?"

"Oh, the *Nutcracker Suite*, *Piano Concerto No. 5*, *Swan Lake* . . . "

"That's a good start. How did you get acquainted with them?"

"I had a student job in the music room at school where I worked two hours a day. It was the easiest job I ever had. In fact the hardest requirement was that I had to play records continuously. Every music major had to spend at least two hours a week there listening to it."

"It sounds easy enough. How long did you do it?"

"One quarter, which was all I could take. The music collection was limited, and after hearing everything over and over I couldn't take it anymore—especially being cooped up with the music crazies."

"Why do you call them that?"

"They were all either too weird or too wild for me."

"Let me play some of the music that will be played at Tanglewood tonight. This is Tchaikovsky's Symphony No. 6, or *Petite Symphony.*"

We settled back, drank our Cokes, relaxed, and heard some great music. I really couldn't believe this girl. Here she was, much older than I—at least twenty-five, damn good looking, smart, and showing a real interest in me. Somehow we got all wrapped up in the music, and before I knew what was happening, we agreed that we would go to Tanglewood together tonight. Carm didn't want to go because of her ankle, and she wanted to be with Ted whom she knew from last year, anyway. So I got the opportunity to escort Jean. We didn't have advance tickets, but that meant we could lie out on the grass on a blanket and enjoy the music with the other young people.

After leaving Jean for the moment, I proceeded to the staff dining room where I learned that I had missed out on one of the big events of the season. The softball game had been a disaster. Mario had always been against letting outside teams in Handover, and objected to today's game, but Williams had persuaded him to let the town team play. Things went well until about the fifth inning when everyone was about soused from the free beer. Several guests were heckling the visiting team, and tempers got out of control. Finally, the visiting team's third baseman went up into the stands after a guest, and it ended up with both players and guests fighting all over the field.

Bodies were bruised and teeth were broken, and the visitors, threatening to return and wreck the place, were escorted by police off the property. Mario was at the hospital commiserating with an injured guest. Earlier, right after the fight ended, he fired Williams.

J.T. and I celebrated the whole episode with a cold beer.

"You know those damn waiters had it coming to them. The cocky bastards think they're the best softball team in New England," said J.T.

"Well, that's what happens when you get to be too big for your pants."

"Somebody told me that those guys from Pittsfield were really good ball players," I said. "I was playing tennis and missed them."

"They were. I saw the first two innings before I had to drive into town, and they had a super infield. And terrific hitters. One guy hit a ball all the way to the swimming pool."

"Damn, that's at least 400 feet. But what about the fight—did you see any of it?"

"No, but Jake told me that Max got knocked down and some guy kicked him in the gut. Jake said that when all those people got on the field, he ran off and watched."

"Crazy Jake is smarter than I thought."

"What happened to you? How did you miss all the action?"

"Let's just say that I was improving my culture and education, and will be continuing to do so throughout the week."

"You lucky shit. You've *scored*."

Well, to be honest, I've come close but haven't scored yet. Maybe this time."

Jean got us a ride to Tanglewood with a guy named Steve Henderson. I had seen him at the pool, but never at the Tally-Ho. Steve stayed at Handover only to go to the cultural events, carefully avoiding the resort's social activities. At first I thought he was really weird. He sat by the pool most of the day reading and drinking scotch, but I later learned that he had been a point man with an infantry company in Europe during World War II. You got the feeling that he felt lucky to be alive, and intended to enjoy a long, quiet, comfortable life.

We took the back way and enjoyed the beautiful New England scenery (I recalled that Robert Frost wrote poems about it). We passed several homes of millionaires who built here in the 1920's. What luxury they must have enjoyed, but now some of these opulent homes had been put to more practical use. One home became a monastery and another a retreat for senior citizens.

We arrived 45 minutes before the concert, so were able to find an excellent place for listening and enjoying the scenery. Jean knew just the spot, for she had used it many times before. I still didn't know what she expected of me, but I certainly enjoyed being with her.

Tanglewood had experienced tremendous growth over the years, and the crowd for a Tchaikovsky program was always particularly large. The seats in the auditorium had been sold out well in advance, and those tickets that were available only allowed you to sit outside on the grass. The auditorium was actually a shed with open sides that seated 6,000, with usually that many or more outside for a concert.

The first part of the program was Tchaikovsky's *Piano Concerto No. 5*, followed by the *Overture from Romeo and Juliet* and the *1812 Overture*. The pianist was a brilliant new discovery who was to conquer all known musical worlds, so Jean said. We were surrounded by people, but we still had a feeling of privacy since those around us were also entranced by each other and the music. And Jean was a terrific hand holder. I can't fully describe what she did or how she did it, but when she kissed my fingertips, I was ready to roll up in the blanket with her for the night.

The *1812 Overture* brought down the house. I was so high on the music and hand holding that it was difficult to stop short of attacking Jean at intermission. The chemistry was fantastic, and I couldn't keep from touching her, and she loved it. We met with Steve for a cola during intermission, and he gave us a lecture on the technique of the pianist. I tried to listen to what he had to say, but Jean wanted to walk around the grounds before the program started again.

The night was perfect for strolling. The old oaks and formal gardens were even more beautiful in the moonlight. As we reached the lower level of the garden terrace, I put my arm around her waist and pulled her close. Without hesitation, she put her arm around me with her head on my chest as though we had done this many times before. I had never met anyone who was so exciting. The music, the grounds, the girl—everything was perfect. We walked on to the big oak in the center of the garden. The oak was surrounded by a low wall, where I sat down and pulled her close to me.

"You are truly beautiful tonight."

"Oh, you Southern guys know how to turn a girl on."

"It doesn't matter where I'm from, this place and you are perfect."

"Do you really like it?"

"I've never been happier in my life."

"Do I make you happy?"

"Extremely so."

"How is that?"

"The way you kiss my hand; the way you let me hold you, like just now when I put my arm around you. You came close and put your head on my chest."

"Don't all girls do that?"

"Not the ones I've known."

"The music excites me so."

"Do you liked to be kissed?"

"If you don't kiss me, I'll have to trade you in for a Yankee."

There are sloppy kissers whose lips are like Jell-O, and there are sweet kissers who make it short, but never had I met such a fantastic kisser as Jean. At first it was very soft, slowly moving in small ovals around the outer lips, then gradually relaxing the lips with a little pressure, and finally slowly opening them for a sensational finale. After several repetitions of this process my body became rigid. I pulled her to me with my head on her breasts. Our hearts were pounding. And then she broke the spell.

"I think intermission is about over."

"I don't want to go anywhere."

"We'll be missed."

"I don't care. I don't want to leave this place." But the applause of the crowd brought us back to reality. The conductor was on the podium, and the orchestra was about to begin Tchaikovsky's *Symphony No. 6*.

If ever any music was written for lovers, this was it. I have heard of many ways to prepare for lovemaking, but never had I expected anything like this. Jean was even more fantastic than she had been earlier. If one ever experienced total exhilaration and complete lovemaking with music, I did on this night. Maybe those music crazies back at school have known that all along.

We got back to Handover about midnight and joined Carm and Ted in the library. Steve served us scotch and water and another lecture—this time on the art of drinking scotch. Jean, however, stayed with her Coke, as did Carm. Ted and Carm had been in the library and appeared to have been really involved with each other when we arrived. Her ankle was much better, though she still limped a bit.

I had established a pattern of going to the Tally-Ho each night, but that was the last thing these people wanted to do. Steve's scotch was certainly a pleasant substitute. Although Jean and Carm didn't drink, they were comfortable with our doing so.

As the crowd drifted back to the Mansion from the Tally-Ho, the others left and Jean and I were alone in the library. The scotch had really taken effect. It wasn't like drinking bourbon; it seemed to have a burning sensation that stayed on and on. I was feeling great and wanted to take up where we had left off on the blanket.

"Would you like to hear some more music?"

"I would like to make Tanglewood on the blanket last forever."

"Let me play some Brahms for you."

"What did you have in mind?"

"Here it is, *Symphony No. 1*; you will especially like the third and fourth movements."

Once the music started she was even better than at Tanglewood—completely loving, soft, and warm. She was right: I did like Brahms. I had heard it many times in my old job at the music room. The scotch, the music, the fantastic kisses—I was now ready for a different kind of finale.

"Why don't we go to your room?" I asked.

"I couldn't do that. Carm is there with Ted."

"How about going out to the pine grove on a blanket?"

"It's too cold out there; anyway, that's a little too *adolescent* for us."

"Look, I can't go on like this; you're just too much. I want to hold you, kiss you, enjoy you to the fullest."

"I want to enjoy you too, but I won't go all the way."

I found that only momentarily disconcerting.

"All right, but I still want to love you more than we can do here."

"I know a place we can go that's warm and private."

"Where's that?"

"Come on, I'll show you." In the two months I had been at Handover I had worked in many places—the Mansion roof, drainage field, and all the cottages, but Jean led me to a room I never knew existed. It was the room where housekeeping items were stored, and was warm, dark, and private. I didn't want to ask how she found out about it. Our destination was a stack of old mattresses by one of the windows. The music from the Carriage Room wasn't as romantic as Tchaikovsky, but after a short while we didn't notice the difference.

There was just enough light coming through the window to make everything exciting—form without detail. We entwined on the mattress and started the soft, gentle kissing we had enjoyed in the library. I wanted to encourage her to go on to more involved things, but she didn't need any encouragement. The scotch, the music, and the darkness converted tenderness into passion. I was on top of her, holding her with all my strength, kissing her as violently as I could without hurting her. She trembled beneath me and almost pushed me off with a rising pressure of her hips.

"Oh Claxton, I can't . . . I can't."

"Please let me."

The blouse, the skirt, the bra came off easily and quickly, but the panty girdle couldn't be moved. Avoiding a struggle for now, I lowered my pants and got a rubber out, and with shaking hands had a hell of a time getting it on. But she wanted no part of that.

"Please just hold me and kiss me."

So I did take her in my arms, and enjoyed the longest and deepest kiss that I had every experienced. She took my erection between her thighs and moved her hips in a fantastic simulation of intercourse. This surpassed any form of petting I had ever experienced. I had a convulsive orgasm, and I think she had one too.

When we both came back to earth there was hardly a word spoken for a long time. I held her close and dozed off for awhile.

The Carriage Room had grown quiet as I was awakened from my dream with soft caresses.

"You are wonderful to love me as you did without getting angry. I couldn't go all the way because then I would have nothing else to give you, ever."

"I don't think I could take going all the way with you. Just petting with you damn near wipes me out."

"Do you want me to tell you why I can't go all the way?"

"If you want, but don't feel you have two."

"There are two reasons. First, there is someone in my life that I care for very much. I hope that we can be married, but several things are keeping us apart. His name is Peter; he's Jewish, and as you probably know, I am Catholic."

"But what does that matter?"

Religion *doesn't* matter that much to me, but it does to his family. They insist that he marry a Jewish girl, so Peter is constantly torn between family and me."

"Do you really love him?"

"On yes, but I get impatient with him when he won't stand up to his family and make his own decision. That is one reason why I'm here this week. We had planned a trip to the coast together, but I realized that all he really wanted was to go all the way and figured I would weaken when we were alone."

"Are you telling me that you're holding off until he promises to marry you?"

"In a way, yes: but that's not all there is to it. I thought he was the only one for me until I met you. You're wonderful; your arms are so strong, and I can feel every movement of your body when you hold me."

"Well, you make me feel fantastic. I reach a point where it feels so good that I just can't control myself. I want to feel the magic of being in you and letting you share how wonderful I feel."

"I know, I know; and I want to, but I'm so afraid of becoming pregnant."

"That won't happen if I use something."

"I know that, but there is another reason."

"If you want it, what reason could there be?"

"It's not easy to explain, but it's something I understand that happened to me, and it will never happen again."

"Are you telling me you were raped?"

"No."

"You're a virgin?"

"No."

"What else could it be?"

"There was someone in my life several years ago whom I thought to be very important at the time. We had been high school lovers, and I thought we would be married after we graduated, but he didn't want to marry. I thought it was the job situation and responsibility that frightened him, but I soon realized that he didn't want to marry me because he had me whenever he wanted without the responsibility of marriage."

"That seems easy enough to stop."

"I thought so too, but then came the real shocker. When I told him we were through, he said he had caught V.D. and would tell everyone he got it from me unless I continued to have sex with him. I was frightened to death at the thought of having to go to the health department for shots, and for my family to know. In my stupidity I believed him when he said he had medicine that would cure us. For some time I let him have his way, out of fear. Nothing, absolutely nothing, can be worse than for someone to have that control over you."

"How did you ever stop it?"

"I was badly hurt in a car accident and had time to think during the recovery period. I made the decision that, since I did come close to being killed, I could now face anything, so I called his bluff."

"How could you ever want to make love to anyone again?"

"Love is the key; no one enjoys it more than I, but I only go so far. Please stop talking about me; kiss me and hold me the rest of the night."

I was able to slip into the tent before J.T. got up for breakfast, but with Jean and the storage room and Tanglewood my sleep was likely to be short naps the rest of the week. The greatest feeling of all was to realize that it was Sunday, my day off.

Since Rand and Monk left, J.T. and I had the tent to ourselves. We managed to keep it a little cleaner, but it still wasn't a showplace. I slept until almost noon, and woke up starving. J.T. had left early to drive people to 8 o'clock Mass, and stayed busy until noon. I was getting dressed for tennis when he finally returned.

"Can you tell me how those people make it to church?" asked J.T.

"What do you mean?"

"Some of them must stay up all night, but they go to church, regardless. I saw two girls smashed at the Tally-Ho last night, but they were ready for the 8 o'clock Mass."

'I guess they need a good dose of church to recover."

I had noticed lately that several of J.T.'s shirts, including the one he was now wearing, had holes in them.

"What have you been doing to your shirts?" I asked.

"You mean the holes?"

"Yeah."

"It's the damndest thing I've ever seen. I couldn't borrow any washing powder anywhere, so I stole some of the stuff they use in the dishwasher. After that they all seemed to start falling apart. "

"Didn't you know it would eat up cloth?"

"I might have asked you what the hell was happening to my shirts, but you've been socializing so much lately that I haven't seen much of you. "

"Come off that shit, you make me sound like Monk. "

"Well, you were out all night, and I'm damn glad you were, because I made full use of the tent. "

"You're putting me on. "

"Really, I did. "

"You had someone here all night? Come on, tell me about it. "

"It wasn't everything I thought it would be, but it was better than what I've done so far. "

"Come on now, who was she?"

"Do you really want to know?"

"Hell yeah, I want to know. Like the waiters, I'll try to move in on you. "

"That's the best part. I put it to someone who had made a fool out of me. "

"How's that?"

"You remember how Red ran his mouth about the nurses back in June when I found him with both of them?"

"Oh yeah, he was the expert—knew it all. "

"Right. Well last night I found the same girl I had here the night you were in the bunk and she cut me off. "

"Damn, you mean the married one?"

"Red's wife, Irene. "

"No kidding. "

"She had left Tent One drunk as a skunk and completely pissed at Red. I left the Tally-Ho about midnight and found her sitting on the terrace steps by the pool. She was ready for anyone and recognized me."

"Why was she so pissed at Red?"

"She later told me that they were getting divorced and he had put the make on someone at Tent One just to embarrass her, so she decided she could play that game too."

"How lucky can you get?"

"Old Monk was right. If you ask enough, you'll find the one who's ready."

"Congratulations, man, how was it?"

"I'll only say this. I couldn't take her every night. I know I'm not a stud, but she made me feel like I was a Valentino. I never dreamed that any woman could make me feel so good. How about you?"

"Crazy, man. Best loving I ever had, but she wouldn't take off that damn panty girdle."

"I've heard that story before. They all seem glued in those damn things. I don't see how they get them down to piss."

"She's really some gal. She doesn't seem to be twenty-four, but she's been out of school for two years."

"Man, you'd better watch out. She's looking for a husband."

"She has someone at home."

"That's what they all say, but if they do have someone waiting, what are they doing here?"

"J.T., you are getting a case of the smarts."

I just had time to finish lunch before I was to meet Jean for tennis. We planned to hit for an hour and head for Tanglewood for the 3 o'clock concert, an all-Brahms program. She looked great on the court. How could she feel so good when she couldn't have slept more than two hours? Maybe going to church did more for you than I thought. My game was terrible, but she poured on the compliments like I was a national champion. She got off on the scholarship bit again and had me believing that I could be in school up here next semester.

Steve, the resident music expert, and Jean's sister Carm drove us to Tanglewood. The concert was fantastic. First, the Boston Symphony Orchestra played Brahms' *Variations on a Theme by Haydn.* Then they played something else, and concluded with his *Symphony No. 1.* Jean was on a cloud when it was over. I liked the music, but it carried her into another world. Neither drink nor drugs could get her any higher. On the way back we stopped for wine at a small inn that Steve knew about. There was a beautiful view of the Berkshires, providing a perfect ending for the afternoon.

Jean, normally a non-drinker, had wine with us. What a day it had been! Now all we had to do was to get back to Handover for the Sunday night buffet and an evening of lovemaking. The guests had already been served, so Jean and Carm ate with us. Steve had been thoughtful enough to get an extra bottle of wine, so dinner was complete.

We were all feeling a little high, but nothing like the rest of the crowd at the buffet. The drinking had grown heavier each week, and the current guests seemed to be the biggest boozers of all. What had started out as a good time had gotten completely out of hand.

Each week at the end of the buffet, the waiters would march around the lawn and select an unwilling soul to be thrown into the fish pond—usually some kitchen hand or busboy—along with a willing guest. This had gone on all summer, and although Mario disapproved of it he didn't want to stop what had become a popular ritual with the guests. The ritual went this way: After one of the kitchen guys was tossed in, the waiters started a chant, "Who'll go next, who'll go next . . .," marching in line to pick out a drunk, willing guest. Usually after a couple of splashings everyone had enough laughs, but on this occasion Max and Fran had to do it one more time.

They chose Red's wife for a final embarrassment, knowing she wouldn't be returning to Handover. Irene put up the usual token resistance until they got her to the pool, and then she stepped out of their reach and started removing her clothes. Off came her blouse, shorts, bra, and panties; and then, "All right, I'm ready."

Max, Fran, and the other waiters were speechless, but after a moment of shock the guests started laughing and applauding. Seeing that the waiters weren't going to toss her in, she jumped into the pool and splashed around, throwing water on everyone nearby. This occurrence, I understand, ended the splashing ritual forever.

Jean and I walked down to the golf course and watched the last rays of sunlight disappear behind Mount Greylock. Haze and smoke settled on the valley as we sat on the terrace with darkness slowly surrounding us. We had finished the last of the wine and were ready for another evening of lovemaking, 1950's style.

The rest of the week went by fast. The number of guests in late August was always small because many people preferred to wait and take a long Labor Day weekend, and so my tennis classes were small. Jean and Carm helped me with them, so we really made progress. Everyone in the class was awed when Jean and Carm would demonstrate strokes. Jean and I also played an hour each morning and afternoon. In fact, we were nearly always together during the week that she and her sister stayed at Handover. With all the tennis and night life, about the only periods away from her were at mealtime. Jean seemed determined that I would be exposed to the cultural events of the week. Knowing I had little money, she wanted to buy the tickets to Tanglewood, but we finally compromised on going Dutch.

Monday night was the Jacobs Pillow Dance Program with Ted Shawn at Lee, Massachusetts. I had always admired the ballet, but had never learned to fully enjoy it. The lead dancer did a circular movement to Ravel's *Bolero* which lasted for at least 15 minutes. I was amazed that he could walk so steadily off the stage. Later on I elicited Jean's wrath by mentioning that the male dancers looked effeminate. She claimed that they were more athletic than I was and that dancing required more rigorous training than tennis or basketball. After seeing the guy completely traverse the stage in two leaps, I had to agree with her. We went to the storeroom for our evening together, but found it locked. With some reluctance she took me to her room, for mostly conversation.

On Tuesday night we went to the theater in Stockbridge to see a Tennessee Williams play, *The Glass Menagerie*. Jean really got involved in the story because she identified her own mother with the one in the play—overbearing and demanding—and monopolized the conversation during the drive back. Jean had studied the characters of the play in a psychology class and shared her knowledge with us all, whether we wanted it or not. J.T. was driving, because guests were provided transportation to the theater, and I could tell that he was making a judgement about Jean that he would pass on to me later.

By Wednesday night I was getting a little tired. Usually I could get a nap after dinner, but every hour of the day was spent with Jean. As a general rule I could usually take late partying because I rested some during the day, but going with Jean both day and night was exhausting. I couldn't understand how she had so much energy. We went to Tanglewood again on Wednesday for a night of opera. The opera workshop group performed *The Queen of Spades* by Tchaikovsky, an opera rarely done according to Jean. I had hoped that we would be able to lie outside on the blanket, but the performances were in the small theater. We were out on the blanket Thursday night for an all-Beethoven program.

Carm and Ted had found another place to go, so we stayed in her room until dawn. What a wonderful night it was. Jean had taught me things about touching that most men never learn. I had even forgotten about trying to remove the panty girdle, for her touch and tenderness far surpassed anything I had ever experienced.

They were to leave on Saturday, so Friday was to be a fantastic day and night. I was ready to stay in New England forever if I could be near Jean. How had I found this wonderful girl out of the hundreds who had been here this summer? She was everything I had ever wanted or desired in a woman. It was really very simple. All I had to do was be accepted by a school up here, and I could transfer at the winter quarter. I'd let Jean make the arrangements for the scholarship, and that's where I'd go. Or even better, I could stay at Handover and work since they were short of help in the fall season. Jean and I could be together every weekend, either here or at her place in Boston. New England in the fall would be great; I'd love to see Boston and the Maine coast.

These were my thoughts as I dressed for tennis. I'd have just enough time to met Jean and Carm at the breakfast bar and make the 10 o'clock tennis lesson. Jean wasn't at the breakfast bar, which didn't concern me all that much because Carm told me she was sleeping in. But when I didn't see Jean at the tennis courts, I suddenly felt lost. We had planned to practice from 11:00 until noon, as we had each day, but she didn't appear. I looked for her in various places after the lesson, but she had completely vanished.

Later in the afternoon I went back to my tent to get some sleep, but my concern about not seeing Jean kept me awake.

The rain started coming down in the early afternoon, and the weather stayed wet and cold throughout the day. All social activities were cancelled except the happy hour, which got off to an early start at 3 o'clock with the Stompers in the Carriage room.

The ground crew welcomed rainy days, for although they were supposed to work around the Mansion, they ended up at room parties or slipped back to their tents. Mike went through the motions of keeping them busy, but he always managed to get in the Carriage Room for a drink or two.

The season was coming to an end; so, with only two weeks left, Mario became lax about staff drinking and working. The staff parties for celebrating the end of the season had already begun, and they got wilder each time. Last night somebody jacked up the side of Tent Seven again, but the staff girls in it were so bombed that they slept through the whole show.

The late hours had taken their toll of the staff and it was beginning to show. Tempers ran short all around. At almost every meal there was an argument between waiters over the serving order in the kitchen.

End-of-season problems were not new to the staff, and things were usually sorted out. The peacemakers usually came forth in time, and the season always ended with a Labor Day weekend to be remembered. I was really down about Jean's disappearance and had stayed in the tent all afternoon.

The rain stopped around 8 o'clock , so the hayride went off as planned. I couldn't believe those guests went out on such a cold, damp night, but after that day's long happy hour, they couldn't feel anything. It could have been snowing for all they knew. The only staff members who went were those who worked at the bonfire or entertained the guests.

At dinner, Stanley invited members of the square dance team to his tent for a party before our exhibition that evening. I went, but remembering my previous visit here before the first square-dance episode, was very cautious with the booze.

We went through the dance routine like professionals. I hammed it up as Mario wanted me to, but it just wasn't much fun anymore. The crowd was so drunk that dancing in squares, or in any organized way, was just impossible. Tally-Ho didn't do anything for me tonight. It had been a week since I had been here, and for the first time this summer I was at the Tally-Ho cold sober. Jean was right about the drinking—there were too many other things to do that drinking interfered with. I started back to my tent, but I had to make one more attempt to find out what happened to Jean and Carm. They hadn't checked out, and were not in their room. Only one place remained where a music lover would go on a cold, rainy night.

The library was even more beautiful with birch logs crackling in the huge fireplace. I wasn't really surprised to find Jean there listening to the music, but I sensed I wasn't going to like what I was about to hear from her.

"Why aren't you at the Tanglewood tonight?"

"Oh, for many reasons."

"I missed you today."

"I missed you too, but I had a full day."

"You really look tired."

"I am.   Carm and I went shopping at Williamstown."

"Carm didn't tell me you were going off."

"I asked her not to tell you because you wouldn't understand."

"No, I don't understand how we could be so close all week, and then you just disappear on your last day here."

"I don't know what you expect of me."

"I don't expect anything. I only want to let things happen, and don't want it to end."

"Please sit down by me and listen to the music; then we'll talk."

She had started *Tristan und Isolde* by Wagner. I sat down and pulled her close. Normally so soft and sweet, she was now tense and unresponsive. We listened to the music which was absolutely beautiful. Without saying a word, we expressed every emotion possible. The music ended, and we sat motionless for a long time. The fire was burning down and needed more wood, but I wasn't about to let her out of my arms, for I knew these were fleeting moments, and I would never hold her again.

"Why does something so beautiful have to end?" she asked.

"I don't know why, but this is the most exciting week of my life."

"I wanted to be with you today, but I had to leave you and try to clear my mind for what I must do."

"Carm told me you were sleeping late."

"I asked her to tell you that, but the truth is Peter called this morning and wants me to come back and marry him as soon as possible."

"But . . . "

"Please let me finish. If I don't tell you now, I won't be able to. I want you to love me in the wildest way imaginable, but I must not weaken because I have a commitment I must keep. You are my fantasy, my high school lover whom I wanted to mold to appreciate the arts as my mother taught me to appreciate them. I wanted to make you into the warm, gentle, loving person he wasn't. I wanted to start my life over and give myself, for the first time, to someone who loved me. I knew from the start that I could teach you to love me because you were so vulnerable and truly innocent, but Peter has changed all that now. He is now what I wanted you to be."

"You were leading me on, playing me against Peter."

"In a way, yes. I've always tried to be involved with more than one person since my painful experience. It prevents being hurt again."

"Let's go to your room and enjoy the rest of the night. Let me love you as never before."

"That would please me so much, and it would be so easy to do but so hard to overcome."

"How would it be different? Just like the other nights, only so much more meaningful. Please don't let it end as just another casual experience at the resort."

"I can't, I just can't."

"If you knew how much I missed you today, how I've thought about us. In my mind, I'm ready to stay here this fall and transfer to any school so I can be near you."

"It would be wonderful, but we still wouldn't be sure. I may lose you to someone else, and I couldn't stand that."

"All I ask is that you let me try. I've only been with you for a week, and look what we've found together already."

"I've dated Peter for two years, and at last I'm sure of him. I can't take two more years to be sure of you. I'm going to my room to pack; we're leaving for Boston in the morning. I'll try hard to forget you, but it won't be easy."

"May I write, or call you sometime?"

"No, please don't. I'm afraid I might come running back to you and lose Peter forever."

"You've given me something I'll never lose—the wonderful feeling of holding someone so close that everything is forgotten."

"I must go now or I'll break all the promises I've ever made."

"Goodbye my sweet, I'll remember you forever."

> *For it's gin, gin, gin*
> *That makes you want to grin*
> *In the corps, in the corps.*
> *And it's whiskey, whiskey, whiskey*
> *That makes you mighty frisky*
> *In the Quartermaster Corps.*

The Carriage Room crowd was in full voice and full of whiskey, and I was catching up fast.

Chapter Eleven

❀ *I Score at Last*

The last two weeks before labor day weekend was staff party time. Every night one of the tents had a farewell party that seemed to surpass the previous one. These end-of-season festivities began on Monday night with Tent Four, which gave a martini party.

Tent Four housed the guys from Tennessee who worked in the kitchen. They were a strange bunch, but threw a terrific party. They were all in graduate school, and two of them had completed their course work toward doctorates in English. On one occasion I had sat in on a discussion of English romantic poets, but they had dismissed me as a mere undergraduate who knew nothing. That was okay with me—I certainly didn't want to be identified with *their* image of the English major. To me they represented the sweet little guys who sat in libraries reading Proust and e.e. cummings.

New England weather in late August can be very uncomfortable, especially when it rains and the temperature is in the forties, but is ideal for parties. The Tent Four party was honored with a rare appearance of Murphy and his wife. They were usually in bed by 10 o'clock, but tonight he was in great form. I couldn't understand how an old man like him—65, at least—could work so long and hard every day. He started nipping in the afternoon, and by dinner time he was high and wild. His temper was unbelievable at times, even to the point of a big argument with Mario about the waiters and serving time.

Murphy was a man of extremes. He either liked you or hated you, and without question he hated the waiters. Some of the waiters made an appearance at the Tent Four party, but disappeared as soon as they saw that Murphy was there.

With the tennis and pool activity limited because of the bad weather, J.T. and I were assigned part time to the ground crew, back with our old friend Mike. We were to work in the Mansion basement cleaning up the storeroom where Jean and I had spent several wonderful nights. After a dull day of rain and goofing off in the Mansion I was ready for any party available—martini or whatever.

I had no experience with drinking martinis. I knew they were powerful, but I thought you would at least enjoy drinking them. My first taste lasted a long time. I couldn't believe anything so universally popular could be so distasteful.

The staff had began to arrive around 9 o'clock, and everyone was high by 10:00. Most of the food disappeared during the first hour, but since Murphy carried the keys to the kitchen, more food was immediately available.

The staff girls who worked in housekeeping were enjoying the party to the fullest. They led a rather neglected life most of the summer since so many girls were already available among the guests. Big Debbie from Mississippi cornered me and announced that she would like to learn to play tennis now that the courts were not used as much by the guests. I really couldn't get interested in her, mainly because she was so big, but also she and her friends had led the cheering at the tennis match with Sara and were still on my shit list. Then too, it would take a lot of drinks to improve her looks.

My second martini tasted a little better than the first, and went down faster. I was beginning to feel the potency of these drinks. Everyone was becoming more likable. An air of friendliness prevailed, and some summer-long hostilities began disappearing.

Denny and Tex from the horse stables came in understandably late—they had to take particularly long showers after work. Tex immediately undertook to catch up with the others at the party. He not only talked and dressed like a Texan, but also boasted that he drank like one. No one could put away martinis as fast. He became the star of the party as everyone watched in amazement, waiting for him to fall flat on his face.

Debbie had left me and gotten into a deep conversation with Denny about Tennessee walking horses and the horse country of western Tennessee. To hear Denny talk you would think that he tucked in each horse at night and served them breakfast in bed. He raved on about the old country and how he grew up with horses, even as a very young boy. He made it sound really good, and she was eating it up, but Murphy had told me that Denny grew up in New York City and had never even *seen* a horse until he came to Handover. Even better than that—Tex was from Albany, New York.

Tex had finished his third martini in 30 minutes, a new Handover record. He then got through the fourth, but not the fifth, at which point he also set a record for the shortest five-drink party attendance at the resort. Several knowledgeable martini drinkers thought that his big mistake had been not to sit down, because that would have slowed his circulation. Others thought that he should have eaten more to offset the gin. But generally no one gave a damn, if he was that stupid. Denny and Debbie awakened him enough to drag him back to the barn. He wasn't seen for the next two days and still looked sick when he tried to eat at the Wednesday night barbecue.

It took me a long time to finish my third and final martini. I still had the clearness of mind to stop while I was in control. Somehow, as the crowd thinned down, the party became a little too intimate for me; not that I oppose closeness and sweet talk and all that good stuff, but I like it with girls. The sweet little Tennessee guys with their high-pitched voices were more than I could take. My martini head cleared quickly when one of them sat next to me and started to rub my back, telling me what a beautiful body I had. Big Debbie had returned from the barn and came to my rescue. She had gone to school with them and seemed to have an unusual relationship. They recognized her as "big sister," and heeded her cautions to "cool it" with straights or someone she wanted.

"How do you like the party?" she asked.

"It's fine, but I'm afraid I'm going to flake out like Tex."

"Don't worry about that. I'll take care of you."

"Please do. I don't think I could stand one of those queers touching me."

"They're harmless, but like everyone else, they want to be loved. Let's go over to my tent and have a long talk about them and why I am so close to them."

Both Debbie and Cathy were from the University of Tennessee. They had shared Tent Seven with Sara before she left. Cathy was an interior design major and had done a beautiful job on their tent. I had only been in it once, the time Sara and I got drunk after our match. Except for Tent

One, theirs was the best looking and they had done an exceptional job of decorating with old, beat-up furniture.

Cathy had used an oriental theme, staying with dark colors. She had painted all the furniture black, spattered with red, giving it a wild look. They had gotten a beautiful silk screen from somewhere that really made the room.

Our tent had only two beds, one dresser, and a lot of clutter. These girls had the beds arranged so they still had room for a low round table and sofa. There was even a rug they had gotten from a remodeled cottage. With beads hanging from the ceiling and the bright colors contrasting with the dark furniture, I felt that I was far from handover and the drab tent I lived in.

"Let me fix you a sweet drink," she said.

"Anything to take away that martini taste."

"They were strong—too strong for poor old Tex."

"I'll bet he'll be miserable tomorrow."

"He's already miserable. I left him sick as a dog with Denny. He'll feel lousy for several days. Would you like a Black Russian?"

"Sure . . . you have the liquor to fix it?"

"I have the liquor to fix almost anything you want," she replied, while opening a cabinet filled with bottles.

"Where did you get all that stuff."

"From the rooms of guests who have left. You would be surprised what they leave behind."

"Aren't you supposed to turn the stuff in to housekeeping?"

"We do turn in most of it, but we keep the liquor and some other selected items."

"What other selected items?"

"I'll show you later. How's the drink?"

"Much better than the martini." I was beginning to feel woozy from the three drinks I'd had so far. "What does this have in it?"

"Vodka, plus kahlua to give it sweetness."

"It won't be too great a change from the gin, will it?"

"I don't think so. The vodka will be strong like the martini, but the kahlua will give a mild, soothing taste."

Before I got started on my drink, she had lit two candles on the table. The scent of the candles along with the colors of the room really gave me an unusual feeling. The drink was sweeter than the martini, but the effect was the same.

Debbie was beginning to look better. She wasn't basically unattractive, just big. She was blue eyed with long, wild blond hair, and spoke a true Southern dialect of Mississippi. I hadn't seen much of her at the Tally-Ho during the summer, but I was soon to find out all the excitement hadn't been at the Tally-Ho. The tent parties had been going on all summer, and those who attended hadn't missed anything anywhere else.

"How's the drink?" she again inquired.

"Delicious, but it goes down so fast."

"Good, I'll fix you another."

"Have you enjoyed the summer?"

"Oh yes, it's been great."

"I don't recall seeing you at the Tally-Ho."

"Well, Cathy and I palled around with the Tent Four guys, and they didn't like going down there."

"Ya'll must have stayed close by and partied a lot."

"We did, but we also went to many events in the area—the theater, the dance festival, Tanglewood."

"Yes, I got to those places too, with a girl named Jean."

"I saw you at the theater with her . . . a short girl, sort of athletic looking."

"She was a good tennis player.   Speaking of which—have you heard from Sara?"

"Yes. She's getting married over Labor Day to the guy she went with. Do you like short girls, like Jean?"

"I liked Jean, but she ran back to her old boyfriend when he offered to marry her."

"I've seen you with several different girls. Do you like to change often?"

"It depends. Usually I don't have much choice, with them leaving every week. Have you gone around with anyone else?"

"Not much chance of that. I stay with the guys from school because they are comfortable with me, and they give me a chance to go places I couldn't go alone or just with Cathy."

"Don't you want more than that? I'd think they would get a little boring to be around all the time."

"They have more to offer than you might think, but they realize the staff girls have strong competition from the guests. When Mario asked the staff to stay on campus and entertain the guests, he didn't intend that for staff girls, only guys. We were told indirectly to let the guests have the guys."

"But Rand and Janet were staff, and had something going all summer."

"They were the exception, but most of us did our own thing."

"What was your own thing?"

"Let me fix you another drink before we get into that."

I didn't need another drink, but how could I refuse? Anyway, the candles and incense were beginning to make my head spin, and the feeling wasn't all that bad.

"Did you hear about our trip to the City?" she asked.

"Only that it was wild."

"Wild isn't the word—fantastic, incredible, is more like it."

"You're beginning to make me feel as if I've had a very dull summer."

"New York was great. You know we made that trip in the old funeral car that Jake bought in Pittsfield."

"How did you manage to work the next day?"

"Very *slowly.*"

"How could you really have a wild time with those guys? I'd think they would probably end up going to the library or museum."

"That's where you're wrong. We went to some places in the Village that were beyond anything I had ever seen or read about. The drag shows were just incredible."

"What's a drag show?"

"Come on, you know what that is. Female impersonation."

"I know about the ones in New Orleans, but aren't they more an art form than a sex show?"

"That's right, but the ones in New York don't hold anything back."

"I don't think I would like being around those queers. They all look and act too freaky for me."

"You'd be surprised. The guys in a gay bar look like guys in any other bar, only they know if you're one of them. I don't know how they know, but they never bother you in any way."

I was trying to listen to everything she was saying, but the drinks were taking their effect—not only on me, but on Debbie as well.

"What can a drag show queer do to turn you on?"

"They can show a big girl something she likes."

"Like what?"

"Like a ten-inch dick."

"You're kidding."

"Oh no, I saw it."

"If those guys are hung like that, why can't they enjoy women more than men?"

"I don't know, but they can make you feel fantastic."

"If they don't like women, how can they show you anything?"

"I didn't say they didn't like women. They just prefer men as lovers. They have taught me what to enjoy as another woman would, and at the same time taught me what a man enjoys."

"Did you learn all this at the drag shows?"

"I learned this over a long period of time, but I saw my first ten-inch dick at the show. Are you that big or just average, since you seem to like short girls?"

"Short girls like big dicks too, but I don't qualify for the show."

I had heard many stories of wild girls at Handover, but before this night was over I experienced the champion. Sometimes you think you have something special, as I did with Yvonne and Jean, but here was something only two tents away that I didn't know existed. All the miserable nights of frustration at the Tally-Ho, and here was pleasure beyond belief only a few steps uphill from my tent.

I wasn't exactly a virgin, but neither was I all that experienced. And my few sexual episodes had all been a struggle—I had certainly heard my share of "stop," "don't do that," "I'm not that kind of girl," et cetera, et cetera. With Debbie, I can't remember what was said or how the action started, but we were undressed and in bed without a single one of those familiar protestations.

I had expected to "lead the way," in the usual male manner, but Big Debbie took control. Her tongue was in my mouth curled around mine, and she was sucking as if to pull my tongue from its roots. She took my hand and placed it on her breast, which had huge extended nipples, while she rubbed my penis and extended her fingers to massage my rectum. My erection may not have been the ten inches she so admired, but it had certainly reached a serviceable length.

When I say Debbie was big, I mean *really* big. How she got on top of me I don't know, but if she wanted to be in control I would certainly go along . . . no protests from me! She was on all fours straddled over me like a female lion playing with its cub. I thought she was ready to grab my dick and put it in, but she wasn't finished with the foreplay. Gasping for breath as our lips and tongues disengaged, she began another game of hanging her huge breasts with their bright red nipples down in my face. I sucked one nipple and then the other, and finally took both of them into my mouth. She placed my hand on her wet cunt an started moving her hips faster and faster. My blurred mind was racing to guess what she would do next as I looked up into her taut, glazed-eyed face.

I should have been thinking about a rubber or how in the hell did I ever get involved in this, my first experience at pure, raw sex, but at twenty who is going to think in these circumstances? She pulled her breast from my mouth and stared at me with those glazed eyes as if locked on a target. The message was, I'm ready and you'd damn better be too. The glazed stare was replaced with a smile of joy as she sat up on her haunches and slowly directed my penis into her with sighs of pleasure, never letting our eyes lose contact. Then she began a bouncing motion that threatened to push me through the bedsprings.

For what seemed like a very long time, my sweat-drenched body reacted with all the vigor of a twenty year old male indulging in a new and exciting sexual pleasure. I met pressure with pressure and force with force until the mighty release could not be contained, and I managed one final gigantic thrust before all my muscles became limp. I was ready to relax, dose off, and maybe try again later. But the lioness wasn't finished.

According to everything I knew about sex, my climax was to end the action. The girl was to give one final scream and maybe pull my hair or bite my neck and then tell me how wonderful it was when the earth moved under her. But in reality, Debbie's energy was far from being exhausted. She continued to twist and push on my pelvic girdle until I was ready to cry "I surrender!" or whatever was needed to stop her. As my penis finally slid out of her with its blood supply depleted, she stopped the grinding and pushing only to wrap her gasping, trembling body around me like a wrestler making a final victorious pin of a beaten opponent.

For the first time in my life, I could honestly say that I not only had experienced all the sex I could stand, but all

I wanted. Handover had given me a four-to-one ratio of women, okay—all in one Big Debbie.

Staff party week seemed to drain the last reserves of strength from everyone. Friday night was the bon voyage party for Herman, the German exchange student who worked as pot washer. Herman had attended Davidson College, but wanted to see more of America than from a Southern college campus. So here he was at Handover.

Everyone was exhausted from the long working hours and heavy partying. I even began to understand and appreciate some of the problems of the waiters and why they goofed off as they did. I had Sundays off and could take it easy on a rainy day, but they worked every day—and *especially* hard on Sundays and rainy days. They made the most money, but really worked hard for it since their base pay was a dollar a day.

The resort workforce was made up of some really interesting people whom I got to know better at the staff parties. I learned that most of the male staff came to Handover for reasons other than the fact that there were four women to each man. Herman wanted to see another side of American life, while the gays had spent all their extra time at the New York City Public Library doing research for advanced degrees. Chris was studying television production at Boston College, and Andy was majoring in international relations at Johns Hopkins. Even the guys from Yale and Princeton were friendly when they got boozed up and came off their high horses. I guess they were there on the theory that rich guys need hands-on working experience too. They all seemed to be determined to be millionaires by age thirty, and I'm sure some were.

Of the four medical students on staff, three had finished the first year of medical school. "Doctor Ray" from Charleston, South Carolina, was the most interesting. He wore a coat and tie to every staff party and refused to let the jokes about his Southern Gentleman dress bother him. He also managed to get something going with Kay from Charlotte, the best looking girl on the staff. Everybody said that Dr. Ray's particular appeal to Kay was the money he was going to make.

Tom O'Callahan was probably the best liked guy on the staff. He traveled in all staff circles, but didn't seem to belong to any clique. Tom was Boston Irish who had played football at Notre Dame and was a fine athlete, as I found out in a tennis match. We played late one afternoon when the New England chill forced us to wear sweaters. I thought I would warm up as the match went on, but just never got hot. I sweated, but the sweat just chilled me more. Tom moved as all good athletes do, never quickly or hastily, but always there with smoothness and complete control. He moved to my wide crosscourt forehand like a halfback running an end sweep—graceful, deliberate, and with exactness. As a halfback would pick the exact moment to make his cut, Tom knew when to hit the return down the line and charge the net like a tiger.

The story was told of two gate crashers who stormed into the lobby of the Mansion and were about to work over the night clerk when O'Callahan came through and wiped them out. Word soon got around town that gate crashers would be thrown out by the new goon squad. There were no further gate crashings that summer.

You would think that Tom would still be connected with athletics in some way, but he was an assistant principal of a private school in Connecticut. He had no interest in coaching or playing, just enjoying an easy, relaxed life. If anyone at Handover seemed to have a handle on life, it was Tom.

One night at Tally-Ho I got down a little later after drinks in Tent Seven, and met Tom's girlfriend leaving. She was so drunk she could hardly walk. I led her to a bench by the gate to the courtyard and went to find Tom. When I told him that she had passed out, he said at least he would know where to find her when he was ready to leave.

Chapter Twelve

 Horses and Rennie

The last Monday of the season started as most of them had—with an announcement over the loudspeakers of the day's events. Mario had replaced Williams, fired after the softball debacle, on the PA system.

"Good morning, everyone. We have a full day planned for you, something for everyone."

"At 10 o'clock on the tennis courts, Claxton Carter will give tennis lessons to both beginning and advanced players. Claxton is Southern Collegiate Champion and an outstanding player. Anyone who needs a game with a good player, see Claxton."

It was 9:30 and I was finishing preparing the courts for the day's activities. Once again, I had to chuckle at Mario's line of bull about my tennis accomplishments.

"Are you as good as Mario says you are?"

"What?"

"I said, 'Are you as good as Mario says you are?'" She was a lovely blonde, with a well tanned body and an aura of style.

"Oh yes, actually much better," I replied, and we exchanged smiles.

"Can you play this morning?" she asked.

"Sure."

"What time?"

"Why don't you stay for the class, and then we can hit. I'll only be with them for about 45 minutes."

"I'd like to, but I've got to make some phone calls. I'll be back at 10:30."

"That's fine. I'll be here." As she departed, it occurred to me that I hadn't asked her name. But I'd find out, soon enough. I turned my attention to the group of guests here this morning for tennis lessons. The group was small, only ten girls. This was in keeping with the house count, which was always low the week before Labor Day.

After ten weeks of these classes, I could go through the routine like an old pro. It was the same old stuff—same questions, same little jokes. New York office girls were being misled into believing they could learn tennis, golf, horseback riding, and even meet the perfect man for only $150 a week—the perfect vacation in the beautiful Berkshires.

The blonde didn't return, and after the lesson ended I looked around for her. She wasn't to be found on any of the other tennis courts or by the pool, so I ended up at the tent completely disgusted. With all the rain and cool weather, our tent had become one big mildew pit. Everything was damp and cold. I resolved that if I ever got back home, I'd never complain about Savannah's steamy summer heat again. Well, probably I would, but at least I wouldn't have to sleep in my clothes to keep warm.

J.T. came in just before noon with details concerning Sunday's big promotion—a reenactment of the Battle of Bull Run, with a big buffet set up for the observers. I knew that Mario was a Civil War buff, but couldn't believe that he would go to all the expense.

"How did you learn about it?"

"The reservation people have been on the phones all morning trying to find rooms for the group. We're booked solid."

"What do you mean, 'group'?"

"Don't you know? The people from Manassas, Virginia, who put on these shows. They are some kind of civic club who are Civil War buffs, and they go around as a theater group and put on these mock battles."

"Mock battles? That could involve hundreds of people."

"Maybe not hundreds, but the Manassas group includes fifty people, horses, cannon—all the stuff for battle. They will be here Friday with all their equipment and will stay until Monday. And Mario is picking up the entire tab."

"If those guys are going to be the confederates, where is he going to get the Yankees?"

"Where does Mario usually get the people for the shit detail?"

"You're kidding!"

"I just picked up a whole truck full of Yankee uniforms in Pittsfield. All we need are the cameras to be in the movies."

"Well, I ain't playing no damn Yankee for Mario's show."

"Boy, you really get sensitive about the Yankee bit."

"These people have been good to us, but I think he overplays that Southern role."

"It's all just a big show."

"I know, but I remember the war years when so many guys took training near Savannah. I thought I had enough Yankees to last the rest of my life. They would come into town for the weekend and give the place hell."

"If you had been stationed at one of those bases, you would have done the same thing."

"It's not that. I just got tired of hearing how bad the South was and how great it was up North. The USO would send guys out to stay with us. Most of them were fine guys who were lonesome and homesick. They would stay out most of the night looking for something or just drinking, but my mother always fixed them a good Sunday dinner before they went back to camp. I guess she wanted to treat them as someone might treat her sons who were away in the Navy."

"Did your family grow up in the South?" asked J.T.

"Oh yes, they were there long before the Civil War."

"My family came from Scotland around 1900 to work in the coal mines, but wound up in Georgia working in the marble mines."

"We go back to early bridge builders from England. My mother's family was named Daniels, and many of the early railroads and bridges in Georgia were built by her grandfather. I guess I have a real family dislike of Yankee soldiers because of something that happened to my family during the Civil War. My grandmother told my mother about it."

"Your grandma isn't *that* old, is she?"

"My mother was born in 1894, so her mother was a young child in 1864. Anyway, she said that her grandparents lived south of Atlanta in Coweta County, and late one afternoon a company of Yankee calvary rode up to camp for the night. Since they lived out in the country, there was no resistance at all. Atlanta had fallen, and the Union Army was marching to Savannah. The Yankee calvary was making a wide sweep, destroying any

Confederate forces they could find; and were living off the land. They took all the vegetables her family had put up for the winter, and also all the meat and animals—everything edible except the sorghum syrup, which they didn't like."

"At least they left them something."

"No they didn't. They poured the syrup all over the house, ripped open the mattresses and pillows, and threw the feathers into the syrup."

"The bastards!"

"They could have burned the house, too, but I guess they had some feeling after all."

"Mario is going to pay people to be Yankee soldiers. Glass said that staff, guests, and even gate crashers will be paid five dollars to be in the show."

"That Mario is a showman, isn't he? Imagine spending all that money on something like that."

"Look, they've made more money this summer than they know what to do with. I've carried as much as $25,000 in bank deposits to town, and that's just the small stuff. Mario and Mike carry the *big* money to the bank. It's really simple. All those weeks we were filled up with a thousand or more people; just think, if each one averaged a hundred dollars, how much that would be."

"Wow, and that wouldn't include all the extra things, drinks and so on, which would probably make another hundred per person."

"Right. You see, we work for a piddling salary, and it sounds good to get room and meals, but all that costs very little when you average it out."

"Old Mario has a good nose for business, and he only works three months of the year. Well, I can't complain. I've had a good time."

"Are there any good looking girls in tennis this week?"

"You wouldn't believe one that came by this morning. Best looking woman I've seen all summer. Beautiful blonde with a fantastic figure."

"Was she wearing a light blue outfit?"

"Yes, have you seen her? I let her get away without even asking her name. We were supposed to play at 10:30."

"She went to town with me and wanted to get back by 10:30, but I was held up in the uniform store on our Civil War order from New York. Haven't you heard about her?"

"Come on, J.T., don't tell me someone else is making her."

"I don't know about that, but Fran and Ron have the hots for her, and I heard that they got into a fight over her in Tent One last night."

"She's back, then?"

"Yeah, but you're dealing in hot merchandise."

"So what, let's go eat lunch."

"Staff meeting is planned after lunch for Mario to recruit volunteers for the battle."

"He's sure as hell not going to make me a Blue Belly. I'm Rebel all the way."

"Hi, gang. Go on eating your lunch, and remember, there's more if you want it. Everybody had a good time so far?"

"Yeah."

"Well, I've got something planned this weekend that all of you can write home about, but first let me go over some important announcements. Our housekeeping supervisor, Mrs. Cicarella, wants to remind you of the end-of-season rules."

"Remember, before you leave you must return all linens and your tent must be cleaned up and all furniture accounted for. In the past we've had chairs, mattresses, and even beds stolen. This year your final paycheck and bonus will be held up until you have cleared with me."

"Thanks, Mrs. C. Mike, how about the tent items?"

"Some of you probably plan to come back next year and think that your personal items can be left in the tents, but they can't. We have just enough room in the basement to store things that belong to Handover, and anything else will be thrown away. If we didn't take the canvas tops off the tents, they would be completely ruined by the snow and ice. So if it's yours, take it with you."

"Thank you, Mike. Gang, I want to tell you about the plans for Labor Day weekend. We've had a good summer, and some of you are going to get some nice bonuses, because you have worked hard for them. We want this weekend to be the greatest ever at Handover."

"Here it comes—Mr. P. T. Barnum himself," said J.T.

"I think all of you would like a few more dollars, and at the same time have a good party. I know most of you have an interest in the War Between the States just as I do, since many of you live where great battles took place. This weekend we are having the Virginia Cavaliers from Manassas as our guests at Handover, and on Sunday we are having a mock Battle of Bull Run for the guests. The Cavaliers are a group of historical minded people who put on these shows all around the country. They have their horses, cannons, and uniforms of the Army of Northern Virginia.

"Now, what we need to complete the show is an army of Northerners. J.T. picked up 50 Yankee uniforms today in Pittsfield. Any of you who will be in the Northern army—just for the *show*, you guys from the South—will be paid ten dollars and all the beer you want. I think with staff volunteers and guests who want to participate, we will have a great show and lots of fun for everybody. Ed Glass is in charge of recruiting and training the Northern army."

I couldn't get excited over playing a Yankee, but Ed Glass—the man in charge of reservations—had a long line of guys at his office to volunteer, mostly kitchen help and bus boys who really needed the money. Most of them were one-season people, having worked extra hard on the promise of becoming waiters, but at this point in the season they had given up.

Another small tennis group, about ten girls, showed up for the 2 o'clock class. They were a plain looking bunch of secretaries and office workers who could hardly pay their bills, but wanted to do everything offered at Handover. I was almost praying for rain so we could cancel the class and slip into the happy hour. Most of them were hopeless. They'd never even seen a tennis match, much less played one. And here they were, expecting to learn how to play tennis in a week. I had just begun my routine of "tennis is like dancing" when a vision suddenly appeared before my eyes.

When the tall blonde girl of yesterday came across the pine grove and joined the group, the dying teacher came to life; every shot suddenly became important, every student movement suddenly needed improving.

"Am I too late for any gems of knowledge today?"

"You can either join the group now or wait a few minutes, and I'll hit with you."

"That's fine. I'd really like to wait here and watch you teach."

"I had no idea of her tennis ability, but I sure put on my best teaching show—made sure that shoulders were in the proper position, and checked every grip and follow through. Rennie might have thought that I was direct from a teaching school in California or Florida by the display I put on.

"Okay, girls, that's it for today. Be sure to hit some before tomorrow's class, but try not to overdo it and get blisters on your hands."

"My my, you know your business," Rennie said.

"Thanks, I've been at it for awhile now. I missed you this morning."

"I had to go to Pittsfield to run some errands and couldn't get back on time."

"J.T. told me about it. I'm sure you had enough of the waiting around while he picked up his uniforms."

"If I had known it was going to take so long, I would have driven myself. I'm really sorry I missed your class, and now it looks like it's going to rain."

"Let's give it a try. Maybe we can get in a half hour before the rain starts."

Rennie had pretty good form. She had problems getting positioned to hit the ball, but she obviously had taken a lot of tennis instruction.

"Have you played long?" I asked.

"Since I was eight."

"You hit very well."

"Some days are better than others."

My compliment was an exaggeration, for she mis-hit half of her strokes and the ones she did hit were sprayed without control all over the court. From the mechanics of her strokes, it was obvious that she had good coaching; but she lacked timing and a feel for the ball. I convinced her that she was playing pretty good, but was happy when the rain started falling after about 15 minutes.

"We'd better call it a day, as far as tennis is concerned."

"A little rain won't hurt anybody. I'm just getting warmed up."

"I know, but your racquet could warp if it gets wet. Worse than that, you could slip on the wet surface and hurt yourself."

"All right, but I want us to play tomorrow."

"Fine with me!"

"Do you have time for a drink?"

"Yes, if the maintenance supervisor doesn't catch me. We're supposed to report to him on rainy days. But what the hell, this is the end of the season . . . let's go."

Happy hour had started early and the Carriage Room was packed. Not only were nearly all the guests there, but so was every staff member who could slip away from work. It was as if the staff were trying to enjoy the last hours on a sinking ship. Most people were brown bagging, so the drinks were plentiful and strong.

"What can I get you?" I asked.

"I'd like scotch and soda, but how can we get a drink without a bottle? I thought the bar was open."

"Don't worry, I'll get you anything you like."

Big Debbie and several other girls were at a table at the back of the room. I figured that if anyone had scotch, she would, though I certainly didn't want to get involved with her today. Fortunately, she was of a like mind. With no reference to our recent encounter, she led me to her tent and her stash of liquor taken from the guest rooms.

"Would a pint of Chevis Regal do the trick?"

"Perfect! How much do I owe you?"

"Nothing, it didn't cost *me* anything. Now tell me about your new girl. I hear she's pretty hot stuff with the waiters."

"Come on, don't tell me about the waiters fighting over her."

"It doesn't matter. I don't think any of you guys can give her what she wants."

"What does that mean?"

"You'll see."

Rennie was patiently waiting for her drink, somewhat amazed at the antics of the crowd.

"Do staff members party like this every day?"

"Only on rainy days."

"I don't think they could get much work done if they did."

"They work very hard at times, and party hard when the work is over. Most of them are resting for the Labor Day weekend, then back home and to school. Here's your drink, and here's to a very beautiful girl."

"Thank you, and here's to a very good tennis instructor."

"Not that line. Mario will overhear you and have us playing an exhibition match."

"I'm not ready for that, but I do want to play tomorrow."

"You're on at 10:30, if that's not too early for you."

"It's not early at all, why should it be?"

"I thought perhaps you have a big night planned and would be out late."

"I do have a big night planned, but I'll be in early."

"Well, I hope you have a great time. There are many interesting things to do in the area. How's your drink?"

"Very good. You must be a magician to come up with Chevis Regal on such short notice."

"I got it from one of the staff girls. She has a cabinet of good booze that guests left in their rooms."

"What's her name?"

"Debbie . . . big girl from Mississippi. Know her?"

"Yes, she cleans my room."

"Are you in the Mansion?"

"No, I'm in a cottage. I didn't want to share a room with anyone."

"Let me freshen your drink."

"What do you think I was doing in Pittsfield this morning?"

"I have no idea."

"Take a guess."

"Let's see, you planned to play tennis, so you needed a racquet."

"Close, but not it."

"You need some new clothes for the big evening you have planned."

"Right, I need some new clothes for my date, but not what you are thinking."

"What else should I think? You're going out, and you bought something special for it."

"Something special all right, but my date for tonight is a four-legged creature."

"I didn't know we had any four-legged waiters—two-faced maybe, but that's it."

"The hell with the waiters. Why do you think I'm having a good time here? They aren't around to bother me."

"I had heard they were all crazy over you and I can't blame them for that."

"They're all fakes, all put-ons, all out for the fast buck. Enough about them. I went to Pittsfield to buy some riding clothes. I didn't realize that Handover had horseback riding, and I left all my riding clothes in California."

"Do you really like to ride?"

"It's my favorite sport. I've ridden since I was five years old."

"Did you ever compete in shows?"

"Not in shows, but in steeplechase races."

"You're kidding. I've never seen one of them except in the movies, but it looks dangerous."

"It *is* dangerous, but more thrilling than you can imagine. I made the Southern tour last year and rode in two races in South Carolina and Virginia."

"Did you win?"

"No, but I finished without falling, and that is a considerable accomplishment. I'm going riding tonight after dinner, and I'd like for you to go with me."

"I've never ridden a horse in my life, but I'm willing to learn."

"I'll teach you how to get on the horse, but after that you're on your own."

"Let's have one more drink, and then let me go to my room and get ready for an early dinner. I can meet you around 6:30."

I'd liked to have stayed with her and gotten on a buzz, but she didn't seem to care for drinking. The idea of horseback riding turned her on more than anything else.

The tent was damp and dirty as usual, but I had little trouble getting in a short nap before J.T. stumbled in. I had seen him high, but this time he was out of his mind. Once he fell into his bed, I couldn't get anything coherent out of him except that they had one hell of a party at the lodge. After several attempts to get him up for dinner, I gave up. Sure hope he didn't have to drive tonight. All he would have tomorrow to remember about tonight would be a big headache.

J.T. knew something about riding, since he had lived on a farm in north Georgia, but I couldn't count on him tonight. At least he could have told me what to wear. Since I didn't have any riding boots, I would just wear my tennis shoes, without socks because they were all wet.

Jeans, sweatshirt, and windbreaker would have to do. I finally got my act together about 6:15 and started toward the Mansion lobby to meet Rennie. Her cottage was next to the Schoolhouse Cottage, and I just couldn't get down there in the rain. She had been most optimistic about the rain ending so we could go on the twilight ride, and it looked as if she might be right.

The lobby was packed with drunken guests trying to get into the dining room. All the people who had been seated on the terrace had to wait until tables were available inside. Most of them were beyond any amount of reasoning and would probably fail to notice the rain on the terrace. One loud bunch kept talking about things that looked good when thrown back up—fruit cocktail, for example. Rennie had eaten dinner in the glassed porch dining room that overlooked the pool and October Mountain, the beginning of a mountain group known as Jacob's Ladder. An unobstructed view of Jacob's Ladder gave you the best seat in the house. Rennie came out through the glass doors, and was by my side before I saw her.

"Are you ready to ride, cowboy?"

"Wow, you came dressed to ride in the horse show."

"Just what I'd wear for any ride."

"Well, I don't have any boots or a ten-gallon hat, but maybe I can make it."

"Did you see the view of October Mountain, and the sun breaking through the clouds? I want to ride up there and enjoy the full view."

"We'll try it but it'll take a long time, so we'd better get started."

We sloshed our way to the barn, which was down the hill from the Mansion. The rain had washed more gullies in the road, which made walking in the ditches more difficult. Rennie almost slipped on two occasions, so I had to put my arm around her waist and hold her up. We slipped and slid the last two hundred yards to the barn, but holding her made the walk a pleasure.

The barnyard was ankle deep in water and had a horrible smell, with flies buzzing around by the millions. How anyone could like being around horses was beyond me. It appeared as if Rennie and I were the only twilight riders. We were there at exactly 6:45 as planned, but obviously were not expected judging by the dialogue coming from the barn:

"Get around there, you goddamn son of a bitch! Don't rear up at me!"

"Put that damn head down!"

The horses were bellowing, stomping, and running all over the barn. We cautiously walked to the main entrance to see a sight both comical and disturbing. There in a rage was Denny, the amiable Irish horseman from the old country, who had boasted at the Tent One party of his love for horses. Denny had taken a two-by-four board to the horses who wouldn't go into their stalls. He didn't see us enter until he had just hit one horse in the side with a full swing of the board. Rennie was outraged at what she saw.

"You *stupid* old man, stop that now or I'll run this pitchfork through you. Don't you know you could permanently injure that horse?"

"Who the hell are you to tell me what to do?"

"You don't know anything if you treat them like this."

"It's the only way to get them in the stalls. Anyway, this mare is a mean one."

"She's mean because you're inhuman."

"If you're so smart, saddle up your own horse."

"I'll do that. I don't know who owns these horses, but I'll see that they know you're mistreating them."

"To hell with them. They're all yours." Denny stomped off.

Rennie continued to fume, and I thought our riding plans were over. But she calmed the horses and got them into their stalls.

We had a hard time finding all the equipment needed to saddle them, but Rennie showed she knew what she was doing. In just a short time the horses were saddled and ready to ride, but when I looked at Sam, my horse, I wasn't so sure of getting through the night. He was taller than I—at least fifteen hands high, according to Rennie.

We led the horses out of the barn to mount them. If I had been on Sam inside the barn, I'd never have gotten out the door. He made me sit ten feet high.

"Have you ever mounted a horse before?"

"I've only seen it done on TV and in the movies."

"Well it's really very simple. All you do is place your left foot in the stirrup and spring up on him; or you can hold onto the saddle and jump on him, then place your feet in the stirrups. It's like water skiing—once you learn you never forget."

"But I don't water ski."

"Go ahead and try it."

It took one try for me to agree with Denny—this horse only understood the language of a stout board. Just as I made my spring with my right leg Sam moved, and I ended up flat on my back on the ground with my left foot in the stirrup.

"You must convince him that you know how to ride. They know immediately whether or not you can take control, and if not he will control you."

"He needs another talking to with that two-by-four."

"That's *not* how you do it. You must be firm yet gentle with him."

"Don't you need to lower the stirrups for my legs?"

"No, that puts your knees too low, and you will need them up high."

"I can't sit that cramped."

"You must in order to control him. Let me hold his head while you mount. Remember, the key is to spring up on him, not to pull up on the saddle."

I gave it another try, and amazingly it worked.

"See, you'll never forget how to do that. Now, lean forward with your feet in the stirrups."

"They're too high; my knees are killing me."

"Your knees and legs must stay high because that's how you control the horse's movement and direction."

"I thought the bridle did that."

"Oh no, that only keeps his head up. Use your legs to direct him. And remember, he only obeys if he knows you are in control."

While Rennie was mounting, Sam put his head down and looked up at me. If he could talk, he probably would have said, "I remember you, you son of a bitch. You're one of the guys who chased us out of the lower pasture last June with the pick-up truck. You're the one who hit me on the ass with a rock, and you are a friend of that damn Irishman who hits me with boards. Well, I'll even the score tonight. I'll give you a ride to remember."

"Are you ready?"

"I don't think this horse likes me."

"You've got to make him know you're in control. See, his head is down; keep the reins tight and his head up. Do you know how to get to the trail up the mountain?"

"I've only been up there once to get some firewood, but you follow the muddy road by the golf course down to the old railroad bed. Go down it about a half mile; the trail goes off to the left."

"We'll let them walk down the muddy road and gallop on the old railroad bed."

"Sounds fine, but I don't know about the gallop."

"You'll love it. Just keep his head up and push in with your knees."

We started out in a slow walk. I wanted to ask Rennie more about riding, but she moved on ahead of me and wouldn't look back. Her terms were that she would get me on the horse, and then I'd be on my own.

Before I realized what was happening, she had started her horse in a trot. I held the reins tight and pushed with my knees in a steady rhythm. To my surprise, Sam responded by beginning to trot. This wasn't so bad after all, although I was much higher in the air than I wanted to be, but maybe he was beginning to see who's boss.

Once Rennie reached the old railroad bed, she hit her horse with the extra bridle strap and took off in a fast gallop. Surely she didn't expect me to ride that fast, but what she or I expected didn't count. Sam had taken over.

You would have thought that he was breaking out of the starting gate at the Kentucky Derby. Rennie's horse was about ten yards ahead of me, and Sam was hell bent on catching them. She had told me how to get him started, but said nothing about stopping him.

Sam's sudden burst of speed completely caught me off guard. I knew I should have been leaning forward close to his neck, as I had seen in the movies, but I had almost been thrown off, leaving me straight up in the saddle. His height and my inability to lean forward put my head on the same level as the tree limbs which had grown over the old railroad bed and which were hanging low because of the rain.

Sam knew how to strike back. I had ridden roller coasters and other thrill rides, but none compared with this. Rennie never slowed down, so neither did Sam. All I could see was the back of her horse and the tree limbs coming at me. I tried to duck the low ones I could see, but Sam kept running so fast that I finally grabbed the saddle horn and held on for dear life. After what seemed like an eternity, Rennie slowed down. Sam, through no direction of mine, slowed down too. He went into what Rennie later told me was a cantor. This was even worse on my rear end and back than the gallop. He seemed to use all four feet at different times, throwing me in four different directions.

We had gone past the trail that led up the mountain by about a hundred yards when he decided to go back to his steady walk.

"Wasn't that great?"

"Great? It scared the hell out of me."

"No reason for that. Just think how hard the horses worked to give you that fast ride."

"I didn't know you were going for another steeplechase cup."

"Oh, that's nothing compared to the steeplechase. You need the jumps to really make it exciting."

"Do you still want to ride up the trail to the top of the mountain?"

"Oh yes. Is it much further?"

"We've passed it by about a hundred yards."

"I didn't realize we had ridden so hard and fast. It must be a half mile from where we started."

"At least, and every foot of it filled with danger."

"You weren't really afraid, were you?"

"I'll only say that if you do that again, I'll get off and *walk*."

The ride up the mountain took much less time than I had expected. When we reached the top, the view was just as beautiful as Rennie had said it would be, with the sun going down behind the clouds and the fog forming in the valley. We found a dry place under a big oak tree and just sat and enjoyed the view while the horses rested.

"Do you like working here?"

"It's okay, but I'm about ready to go home."

"What do you miss about home?"

"Well, it's much warmer, and I miss my mother's cooking."

"Is there much difference in the food here? I thought the staff had the same food as the guests."

"We do, but at home we have more fried food, like potatoes and okra, while here everything is baked or broiled. We would never have broiled fish; just fried, or maybe boiled fresh shrimp."

"What else do you miss about your home?"

"My whole family. We're pretty close. How about you? How's your home life?"

"My parents are divorced. My mother remarried and lives in California, and I live with my father."

"Are you still in school?"

"No, I got tired of school and went on tour with the steeplechase."

"You really like riding, don't you?"

"I like anything that's thrilling and exciting—flying, auto racing, as well as horseback riding. My dad lets me do whatever I like if it doesn't cause him problems."

"What does your dad do?"

"You really want to know?"

"Not if it bothers you."

"It does, but I live with it. He's president of one of the largest labor unions in New York."

"Hell, that's quite an achievement. My dad was always a strong union man; wouldn't work any other way."

"You don't understand how unions work. He runs things like a dictator."

"Wasn't he elected democratically, by the members? One of my sociology classes covered union organizations. He's bound by some written rules."

"Your information is like something out of *Alice in Wonderland*. Democratic unions—part of the great American dream."

"Look, this may sound corny but the unions have helped make America great. My dad used to say that without the unions, the working man would be at the mercy of big business. He remembered when a man worked for almost nothing unless he was in the union."

"All of that sounds good, but you don't know about the politics and the crime connected with unions, and how even worrying about it can tear your life apart."

"No I don't, and I guess I don't really want to learn. I'd like to continue the dream that most people are honest and have good intentions."

"You'll learn one day that most people are not honest with themselves or anyone else; that they will pay any price to get ahead and then stay there."

"I'd really like to forget that for now."

"Me too, The view is too beautiful to miss. One the sunset is gone, our view will end for a long time."

"You are really a lovely girl."

"You think so?"

"Absolutely."

We sat there a long time without talking; just looking at the fog and mist, with the sun slowly setting through the clouds.

"Do your parents love you?" I asked.

"They did once, but got caught up in the getting-ahead game, and then forgot about me and each other."

Of all the girls I had met at Handover that summer, Rennie had by far the most natural beauty. We sat there silently watching the last rays of the sun disappear behind a huge, low-lying cloud.

I wanted to take her in my arms and just hold her for hours. As beautiful as she was, I sensed that she lacked love and wanted it. There was a loneliness in her life that

I wanted to fill, but that would have to wait, for it would soon be dark and we had to get the horses back to the stable.

The ride back was much more pleasant that the one out. Since it was almost dark Rennie let the horses walk down the mountain trail, for there was the danger of their stepping in a ditch or hole with bad consequences all around. I wish she had been as concerned about me when we were racing down the road earlier. My back and rear end wouldn't take any more fast riding, but something even more painful was developing. Whereas most people wore boots for riding, I wore only tennis shoes without socks, and my ankles were rubbed raw from the stirrups.

Everyone was gone from the barn when we got back. I guess old Denny had passed out in his room, so Rennie showed me how to get the saddle off, water the horses, and get them into their stalls. Sam was as gentle as a lamb, but if Rennie hadn't been watching I would have whacked him with a board to remind him of my displeasure over the rough ride. But now my thoughts moved on to further things.

"Are you ready for a drink and dancing at the Tally-Ho?"

"I'll take the drink, but let's pass up the Tally-Ho. I'd just like to sit by the fire and enjoy some good music and conversation."

It was almost 10 o'clock when we got back to the Mansion, smelling a bit like horses. The fire in the library was just what we needed. I made a quick trip to the tent to get my scotch and ice for our drinks. When I returned, Rennie was sitting on the rug in front of the fire. The horses had furnished plenty of heat from their steaming bodies when we were riding, and now it was the turn of the fire to ward off the damp chill of the night. She looked like the All-American girl—long blond hair, blue eyes, and great body. With her riding outfit she looked like an ad in a women's magazine.

"How's the drink?"

"Really good. Perfect with the fire."

"It feels good after being out in the night. I'd like to sleep in here because those tents are freezing."

"You mean you don't have any heat, not even a heater?"

"Nothing at all. It's against fire regulations to heat the tents, so Mike says."

"I couldn't stand it. I've had my heat on every night."

"My folks think I have lost my mind when I tell them we have a fire in August. They are suffering in 90-degree weather."

"I think it's great. Sitting in front of the fire is one of my favorite things. Why don't you rub my back, I love it by the fire."

It took some readjusting, but Rennie lay on her stomach and I was beside her on my knees. My back rubbing experience was limited, but one thing was certain—if she wanted her back rubbed, I would give it my best.

"Use a little more firmness, I won't break."

"You mean more pressure on the muscles?"

"Right, and really push down in the lower area."

"Like this?"

"Oh yes, that's great."

It didn't take experience to realize what she liked. I moved my hands up and down her spinal column, to her sounds of pleasure, and then on to her neck and shoulder muscles.

"You are really good. Your hands are magnificent."

"You are wonderful to touch."

"Rub real lightly in my hair and on the back of my neck. Oh, that feels so good!"

It didn't take me long to discover that she wasn't wearing a bra. I hadn't been with a braless girl since Savannah Beach when I was fourteen.

"Would you like to put your hand under my shirt and just rub my back real lightly?" Of course, I got pretty excited at this apparent come-on, and worked my hand down toward her breast. But at that point Rennie cut me off cold, and later on wouldn't even kiss me goodnight when I walked her to her room. She was certainly different from any other girl I had met this summer.

Rennie arrived at the tennis courts at 10:30 as we had planned, and we were able to play two sets before a light rain started. Even then Rennie wanted to continue playing. She was such a gorgeous girl, the kind I use to just dream about. I really couldn't figure why she had picked me from among all the guys here. Her tennis left much to be desired, but so what? My mission now was to make her happy and perhaps enjoy that All-American body.

I had wanted to spend the afternoon with her in her room, but Mike had rounded up all of us to clean up the storerooms in the Mansion. Rennie left after lunch to do some more shopping, and this time drove her own car. I had never seen anything like it as she gunned it down the Mansion driveway like a rocket. It had to be some imported model, British or Italian, and Rennie drove it like she was in the final lap at LeMans. I was looking forward to the possibility of driving it later—there was a foreign movie playing at Pittsfield that she wanted to see, so maybe I'd be behind the wheel at least some of the way.

We swept up a big box of beer cans and used rubbers in the storage room. I'm sure some of them were left there when I was with Jean. Mario had looked down into one of the drains, which had a window to the storeroom and in which someone had put about six used rubbers. He could tolerate the used rubbers in the pine grove, where Mike's crew could dispose of them each day, but this blew his mind. The clean-up was ordered, and all supply rooms in the Mansion were locked.

For some reason I was more tired than I had felt before. There had been other nights when I had drunk more and stayed out much later, so I should have felt well. As the afternoon went by, my head began to hurt and I just felt lousy. We all goofed off as much as possible, and finally I felt so bad that I slipped off early and got into my bunk.

J.T. was running errands in preparation for the weekend, and I was left in the tent alone. Sleep was wonderful, but I slept much longer than I intended. J.T. woke me up at 7:45 in the evening wanting to know why I had missed dinner.

"Seven forty-five? It can't be."

"Well, it is. I would have come back earlier, but I thought you had Rennie out here."

"I'm supposed to meet her at 8 o'clock, but I feel horrible."

"That's the price you pay for a good time."

"Good time my ass. That damn horse scared me to death, and I almost froze riding back. Worst of all, every bone in my body aches. I know that's from riding, but my throat feels like it has closed up. What's that from?"

"You *are* in bad shape. I'll meet Rennie for you if you can't make it."

"The hell with that. I'll be there if I have to crawl."

"You'd better get going, it's almost 8:00 now."

"Would you stop by the lobby and tell her I'm on my way?"

"Sure, lover, but you had better be there shortly or the waiters will cut you out."

"Fuck the waiters. She likes me best, I just know it."

"This car is fantastic. I've never ridden in anything with such pickup."

"You've never ridden in a foreign sports car?"

"The only sports car I ever rode in was a 1939 Mercury convertible that a girl had here in June."

"A '39 Mercury? That's a collector's item now. You need to go to California where *everyone* owns a sports car."

"How fast will it go?"

"I don't know, but I have had it up to 150. I'll show you when we get on the freeway."

"Is it anything like riding a horse?"

"Somewhat, but a little more breathtaking. Would you like to drive?"

"Maybe coming back, if we *get* back."

"Don't worry, I won't open it up if the traffic is too heavy, but we could try it later tonight."

The excitement of the car ride helped me forget my pounding head and sore throat. She had only hit 100 mph, but that was enough to make me forget everything unpleasant and just hope that we would get to the movie alive.

We had difficulty finding the theater because the entrance was in an alley, away from the regular movie houses. We finally got parked and bought the tickets, which were outrageously priced, but Rennie said all foreign movies were high. At first I thought the couples around us were just making out a little. The theater was very small, and everyone was easily seen because there were less than twenty people there. It took a few minutes to get adjusted to the darkness, but even longer to realize what was going on with the couples. We were late and the show had started, so we missed the first fifteen minutes. That was bad enough, but being in French with English subtitles made the story hard to understand. Even more confusing was the fact that the couples behind us were all women.

I wanted to ask her about the all-female audience, but Rennie was absorbed in the film. If I hadn't been feeling so lousy I could have really gotten excited over the movie, for the actresses were doing things I had only read about. But my head was about to split and my throat was so sore I could hardly swallow. The longer the movie lasted, the more miserable I became. Finally I had to go to the men's room to wash my face and try to find something to stop my head from hurting. I stayed much longer than I had planned, but I still felt lousy. When I was able to return, the movie was showing two women in bed making love. And someone was sitting next to Rennie, arm around her shoulders. My first impulse was to leave, get back to the resort as best I could. Then it occurred to me that it might be one of those waiter bastards, and I wanted to knock the shit out of him.

The ride back to Handover was long and quiet. Maybe if I had felt better, I would have understood, but under these conditions I just wasn't ready to listen. Rennie didn't offer any explanation or excuses; she just remained silent. After what seemed like hours, we finally pulled up beside her cottage.

"Are you disappointed in me?"

"Sort of. A little confused. How did you become that way?"

"It's a long story, but a rather common one, I think."

"At times I've felt you've wanted me, at least while you are here."

"You are only temporary, but the emptiness has been in my life for a long time."

"I can understand why you would be lonely after your parents divorced, but why did you choose that way to find pleasure?"

"It's really very simple when you are put into a girls' school at a young age. You are so lonely and afraid. It's easy to be influenced, especially if your surroundings are unpleasant. I was only ten and didn't know it was wrong to let someone enjoy your body. At first I just went along with what I thought was a game, and then I discovered that I liked it."

"Wasn't there any supervision of students at all?"

"Oh yes, but remember we were from fine, rich families, so naturally we were never supposed to think of such things. We were well mannered, intelligent young ladies whose parents had dumped us there because we interfered with their lives."

"How did you get along with your parents?"

"Okay until their divorce. I now realize she found him impossible to live with because he was gone most of the time. She was sleeping around long before their divorce and afterwards didn't remarry because she was getting sizable child support and alimony."

"How did you know she was sleeping around?"

"You *know*, even at an early age. When I was about four or five, we used to spend our summers at our beach house. My father would come down every weekend, but during the week my mother and I spent most of our time at the beach. There was always someone who met her there. They would stay together while I played, and I always knew that I would go to the baby-sitter's house that night.

"Some nights I would stay all night, and they were horrible. The baby-sitter had boys about twelve and fourteen, and after their parents were asleep they would come into the room where I was. My mother stopped leaving me there when I became ill at the sight of the house. She started getting someone to stay with me when she went out. She usually came home early to make sure I was asleep and let the sitter go home. I would lie awake in my bed hoping that she would let me come sleep with her, but there was always someone else who would slip in the house and go to her room. My room was across the hall, but I would watch them through a crack in the door. They always left the light on and did a lot of grabbing and twisting and turning. I didn't know what they were doing, but if it was anything like what the boys did at the sitter's house, I didn't want any part of it."

"So you dislike men?"

"No, I just enjoy women more. Let's go into my room, this car is getting too cramped for anything."

Handover had given me many surprises, but nothing to compare with what I was about the experience.

"Get undressed while I get ready."

"What do you mean, 'get ready'?"

"You'll see."

I sat on the side of the bed for a few minutes trying to evaluate what she had said. No woman had ever told me to get undressed. She might be a little strange, but this was one experience I didn't want to miss. If only I felt good instead of so lousy. I got undressed except for my shorts and sat on the bed waiting for Rennie. I always thought you took the shower after the lovemaking. Finally she came out wearing only a thin robe.

"I thought you were going to get undressed."

"Well, almost."

"I meant everything."

She had two scented candles which she lit while I slid off my shorts.

"I want you to use this oil to rub me as you did last night. Start off firm, then do as I tell you, and we will have a good time."

She took off the robe and lay on her stomach with her head at the foot of the bed so I could easily reach the full length of her body.

"Use the oil generously."

Her body was gorgeous—firm and trim, but the skin soft as a baby's. I started on her lower back and rubbed firmly on the muscles around her backbone.

"Use a circular motion as you move up . . . oh, that's great."

I did all the things she liked to her shoulders and neck that I had done before. She seemed to drift into a hypnotic sort of pleasure.

"That's fine. Now move down to my butt and use the same circular motion with plenty of oil; then rub real lightly all up and down my thighs."

Without another word she turned over, held my wrist, and moved my hand lightly all over her body. After several minutes of the light touch, she pulled me between her spread legs. With one hand she moved my head from nipple to nipple and used the other hand to rub herself. Sick or not I got an erection, but every time I tried to put it in her she twisted away and shouted, "no, not that!"

I held her as tight as I could, and her movements became shorter and strained, as did her breath.

"*Go down, go down!*"

What in the hell did she mean, "go down"? I wanted to go *in*. The excitement was too much. I couldn't hold it back any longer as the hand that moved me from nipple to nipple firmly pushed my head down, down . . .

Chapter Thirteen

❀ *Hospitalized*

"You've got an infection in your throat," the medical student told me.

"How do you know, Ray?"

"There's white colored tissue in there."

"That's what's causing all the pain?"

"Yes, and it's going to get worse. You seem to be running a temperature."

"I'm so hot and sore I can hardly stand up. I've tried all the medicine for gargling, but none of it does any good."

"Go to a doctor, get it treated. Also find out what caused it."

"What do you think it is, Ray?"

"I really don't know, but the only other case I've seen like this was in Charleston, and it was caused by too much fucking."

"Well, we'll have to find another cause."

I went back to the tent and to bed. My temperature must have been over a hundred, and my throat was so sore I couldn't open my mouth. J.T. finally came looking for me and wasn't surprised to find me in bed.

"What the hell are you doing back here? Mike is looking for you to give Colonel another bath."

"Fuck Mike and Colonel."

"Don't say that or you'll lose your bonus."

"I don't give a damn about the bonus. Ray said I have an infected throat and should get to a doctor."

"He should know if he is in medical school, but half the staff is sick with colds because of sleeping in those wet tents. Mario should let us stay in the Mansion since the crowd is so small."

"Can you drive me to the doctor? I've got to do something. I feel like I'm going to die."

"I'll have to check in with Mike, but we'll go anyway."

They put me in a private, isolated room—no visitors or telephone calls. As tired as I was, I couldn't sleep or rest. J.T. had first taken me to a woman doctor in Lenox. She looked at my throat but wouldn't do anything for it. She said she was afraid it might start bleeding, so the best thing to do was to send me to an ear, nose, and throat specialist in Pittsfield. He was as noncommittal as the first doctor had been, only he wanted me to stay in the hospital for a couple of days so he could run tests to determine what was wrong with me.

Mario got very disturbed when I told him what the doctor wanted to do. Somehow his insurance only covered employees if they were in an accident or stayed in the hospital more than five days. If I hadn't been so sick I would have thrown a punch at the bastard. His wife realized how bad I felt and told me to get to the hospital as soon as possible and not to worry about the bill.

J.T. drove me to the hospital, and his was the last friendly male face I was to see for three days. I lay in bed all afternoon trying to sleep, but each time I dozed off my throat closed up and I would wake up coughing. They brought me some food around 6:30, but I couldn't swallow it. I drank the liquids and began to worry why they didn't do anything for me.

The only good thing of the day was the back rub a good looking nurse gave me. She also gave me a sleeping pill to put me out for the night. I didn't remember anything until someone was waking me up at 6 o'clock the next morning. They had scheduled me for lab, and that meant specimens. I didn't mind the blood test or pissing in the bottle, but I thought they were going to kill me by cutting the culture from my throat.

Back in the room, I tried to sleep because the lab results would not be available until noon, when the doctor would have a conference with me. In the meantime, I couldn't have any food or liquid because it might be harmful. I remembered all the mornings I had wanted to sleep late, and now that I had the chance, sleep was impossible.

The doctor arrived in the early afternoon and told me that I had "trench mouth," a highly contagious disease that can be caught by drinking from a contaminated glass or even kissing. He was a little baffled by the infection in the lower throat but felt that penicillin would clear it up in a day or two. He wanted me to stay in the hospital one or two more days for observation.

What none of us knew was that I would have a strong reaction to the penicillin. The same nurse who gave me the back rub and sleeping pills gave me the penicillin shots as the doctor had directed. At first I blushed a little when she told me that she would give them to me in my rear end, but she assured me that my behind was probably like most others she had seen. She had done a great job on my back, so I believed that she could give shots equally well.

The shots didn't hurt as much as I thought they would, and she was most reassuring that the penicillin would clear up the infection. Until now no one had asked if I ever had a reaction to penicillin, so the nurse said she would keep watch on me in case I had a mild reaction, which people sometimes do.

I was reading the latest *Time Magazine* and found an article about the Democratic National Convention very interesting. The floor fight between the Stevenson forces from Illinois and Jack Kennedy of Massachusetts had really produced some fireworks at the convention. Kennedy had lost to Stevenson, but the article praised Kennedy as one of the promising Democratic Party hopefuls. He had been in the thick of the World War II fighting in the Pacific, becoming a real hero of a real war. Now guys were going to Korea, not to a war but to a "police action." The Marine Reserve Unit from Savannah was called to duty and was on the front lines six weeks later. Some of those guys had been in high school with me and were no more trained to fight than I was. They were taking rifle training aboard ship going to Korea. At times I felt guilty about being in school and deferred from the draft, but my parents had lost two sons in the war and could not bear to lose another.

My thoughts faded into a light sleep which was to last much longer than I wanted. I could hear voices and see figures around me, but they were all in my dreams, so I thought.

"Do you think he is having a reaction to the penicillin?"

"I don't know, was he tested?"

"No, I don't think so."

"Isn't swelling of the lips and ears characteristic?"

"But why is he unconscious?"

"Was he tested for diabetes?"

"Surely he was. I see nothing on his chart about a diabetic history."

"You had better get the interns immediately."

"Has his doctor been called?"

"No."

"My God, sound Code Blue!"

People were rushing in and out of the room. Some were pulling on my arms; others were looking down my throat and giving me all the attention I had missed yesterday. What a wonderful dream this was, only my throat was hurting again, and it was hard to get my breath. Then suddenly the dream ended. I couldn't breathe, and the room turned dark.

"Can you hear me, Claxton?"

"Wake up now, Claxton, wake up."

"He's coming around."

"You really gave us a scare for awhile."

"Am I still dreaming?"

"Oh no, you're going to be fine. You just need a day's rest, and you'll be as good as new."

"What happened? My throat is so sore."

"You had a reaction to the drugs we were giving you for the infection, and it caused severe swelling in your throat."

"Is that why I couldn't breathe?"

"Yes. We had to give you a different drug to counteract the swelling, and we had to use emergency methods to keep you from choking."

"What do I do now?"

"Just rest and let the drugs do what they are supposed to do. I'll see you in the morning, and then you can go home."

The combined effect of all the drugs was to make me sleep like a baby. I hardly woke up to eat dinner, and even though I could swallow the beef broth and drink the liquids, I preferred to sleep. My body was reacting to the late hours it had kept and took full advantage of the rest it needed.

J.T. picked me up about noon, and I was still so sleepy that I could hardly make it from the car to my bunk.

"I saw your late girlfriend checking out this morning."

"Rennie?"

"Yeah, the one all the waiters liked."

The news about Rennie jolted a little energy into me. I had to see her before she left, if she hadn't already gone. But the walk over to Rennie's cabin was still a difficult one. The doctor told me that I would be light-headed because of the drugs and that I should get a lot of rest for a day or two, but I wanted to see her again in hopes that I was wrong about her. Her car was still parked by the cottage, and even though I didn't expect her to be there, I knocked on the door anyway.

"Who is it?"

"Claxton. Can I see you?"

"Can you come back later?"

"No, I need to see you now."

"You'll have to wait."

"I'm not going to wait. I'm here and I want to see you."

Rennie hesitated for a short while and then opened the door. Her face and body were flushed, her hair was tangled, and she was wearing the same thin robe she wore the last time we were together.

"J.T. told me you checked out this morning."

"I did pay the bill, but I have the room until this afternoon."

"I wanted to see you again and tell you that I could really care for you if you were willing to make some changes. You know I was in the hospital for three days."

"Yes, the word got around."

"Did you know I had a reaction to the drugs and almost died?"

"Yes, I heard that, too."

"They gave me a great back rub. I can see why you like it so much."

"You are beginning to live, then."

"I'd like to give you another rubdown and do something exciting, but I'm too weak and sleepy for anything."

"That wouldn't be possible now."

"Could we keep in touch, and maybe if you come back next summer, we could work something out? I know I could care very much for you."

"There's nothing to be gained by keeping in touch, and I know I won't be here next year, or ever again. As for us, you are like so many guys I've known. They want to love me, but it's always what they want. None of you ever consider what I want."

"What do you want?"

"I just want to be satisfied. I have no interest in pleasing someone else. You take those stupid waiters, falling all over themselves about me, all of them wanted me only for their pleasure. Like all other men in my life, they thought they were in love with me. So, I'm going to

California where I can find what I want—men who will please me, not fall in love with me and want to change me."

"Does that include women too, like the ones in the movie we say?"

"That's right, it does. Debbie, come out and say hello to Claxton."

"Hi, Claxton. I told you that you couldn't give her what she wanted."

"I thought you were the one who liked a ten-inch dick."

"Oh, I do, but I like Rennie, too."

Chapter Fourteen

 Our Battle of Bull Run

On the final Saturday morning of the season, the Mansion was a madhouse. Twice as many people were arriving as reservations called for. Mario had adopted the policy years ago that he would find you a room somewhere, even if you had to share a tent with staff.

I had stayed in bed all Friday afternoon and slept most of the night as a side effect of the drugs. Once or twice I had been wakened by Rebel yells; the Virginia Cavaliers had arrived and were starting their weekend party, which lasted through the night. The bed rest worked a miracle. I felt great and was starved. While everyone was hung over from Friday night, I went to breakfast early and ate a huge meal. Three days of a liquid-only diet had me famished.

A few of the waiters came in late, and as usual were bragging about their latest conquests. However, some seemed nervous—a few girlfriends had showed up unexpectedly. Fran, the Adonis, had lined up two earlier summer scores and then his college girlfriend arrived for a surprise visit. She went to his tent where she had stayed on previous visits only to find Fran in bed with his second date of the night. After all the hell raising stopped, Fran had lost *all* of his girlfriends and was unable to work the next day.

Seeing that I was up and about, Mike wasn't about to let me rest anymore. He was short of people, so he put me to driving one of the station wagons, taking guests and their luggage to their rooms. The standard tip was 25 cents a bag, even if it was on the fourth floor of the Mansion. I never thought I could carry four suitcases at once, but when you realize you could make a dollar in ten minutes, it was a breeze. Good money, and you met the women early.

I was a bit weak when I started the day, then my fifth trip to the top floor of the Mansion took all the steam out of me. I had made five dollars, so decided to rest awhile. The balcony above the pool was a great place to enjoy a Coke and look over the new girls, while hiding from Mile.

If the crew around the pool was any indication of what the rest of the weekend was going to be, we were in for a wild time. Half of them were already high, and it was barely lunchtime. At this pace they would be wiped out by happy hour. Mike had mentioned that the Labor Day crowd was always rambunctious and looking for the last fling of summer.

When I came back to the lobby I had a pleasant surprise. Parked in the circle of the Mansion was a familiar and beautiful sight—a 1939 blue Mercury convertible. And then a warning light went on in my head. Was I also to be a victim of multiple returning girl friends? While I was pondering the possibilities, Ann came from the lobby to get her luggage. She saw me and smiled.

"Are you the young man who's going to help me to my room?"

"I can't believe you came back after the last time."

"Let's forget that and start over again."

"Are you going to be here all week?"

"No, just the weekend. I almost didn't get a room. They only had a small single left in the Mansion for me. What's going on, anyway? I could hardly drive in because all of the roads were filled with horses and cannon. Are they shooting a movie?"

"Mario has some mock battle planned for tomorrow, and those people you saw must be the guys from Virginia who are putting it on."

"I hope it's better planned than the air attack thing."

"It had better be, or Mario will have somebody's hide."

"Can you park my car and take my bags up? There's something I need to tell you right away. All I have are two bags on the back seat."

I got the bags out and started to park the car, but all the spaces around the Mansion were filled. The only place I could find was by my tent. Gosh, the car drove great—gutted muffler, straight shift, everything that goes over at school. I had been so excited about driving the car that I had forgotten to ask about the absence of Frances, who happened to own this car. Why would she let Ann drive the car up by herself? Maybe that is what she wanted to talk about, or maybe she wanted to tell me something I didn't want to hear. Ohhhh shit, surely not *that*. I knew I was careless, but not that careless. I had used a rubber both times.

She was waiting on the steps, but somehow she looked different. All business, and no time for pleasure.

"Where did you park the car? It sure took you long enough. I had to fight off three drunks while you were gone."

"The parking lot was full, so I had to go back to my tent to find a place. Now let's take your bags to your room." She headed toward the front door, "No, let's go the back way, it's shorter," I said.

"Don't you want to be seen in the lobby with me?"

"What's the matter with you?"

"I'll tell you when we get to my room."

"I'm not sure I want to go to your room."

"Well, you were never reluctant before."

I know how a condemned man feels walking to the gallows. There are thirteen steps on the first level and fourteen on the second level to the balcony, and then ten paces down the hall to room 207. I closed the door and placed the suitcases on the bed.

"Come here and let me give you a big kiss," she said.

"Where's Frances? Did she come with you?"

"We'll get to that in a minute. For now I want you to hold me and make me feel comfortable and secure."

"What do you mean, 'secure'?"

"That you want me and would stand by me when I need you most."

"Oh shit. I knew it."

"Knew what?"

"That you're going to tell me you're pregnant."

"What if I am? What do you plan to do?"

"It can't be."

"What if it is?"

"Look, the only time I was careless was the first time, but I still had the rubber on."

"You weren't careless, you were ineffective, but I loved it."

"You mean you're not pregnant?"

"It would be a miracle of biology if I were. It was my first time, and I was scared to death, but you were so drunk you couldn't do anything. You'll never know how disappointed I was after choosing you for my first experience and working the nerve to go through with it, and then you didn't perform. I think the problem was what they call premature ejaculation. "

Never was man happier at sexual failures. I heaved a vast sigh of relief, and promptly forgot any lesson I might have learned:

"Give me the biggest kiss I've ever had, and another chance. "

"You crazy man! Hold me, kiss me, love me all afternoon. "

"And all night, too. "

"As long as you like. "

The afternoon was fantastic. The doctor couldn't have ordered any better therapy, but it was cut short by the news of Frances. She had been knocked up back in June by one of the guys from Pittsfield. He wanted her to marry him and have the baby, but she wouldn't consent. She felt that he would leave her after the baby was born and it would be best to have an abortion. She just couldn't face her family and friends. This way she could keep her job and try to straighten out her life. The big problem was that she didn't have the money for the abortion. After the vacation her savings were gone, and unmarried teachers are not covered by this kind of hospitalization. Her only means of raising any immediate cash was to sell her car. What rotten luck—no money and pregnant, and without the abortion, no more job.

Ann said that I could have the car for three hundred dollars, but it had to be cash and I would have to get it by Monday. She knew I wanted the car, and Frances had to have the money next week. She was right about my wanting that '39 Mercury. For the first time I can remember, sex wasn't the most important thing in my life.

"Well, Claxton. Good to see you back in shape again."

"Thank you, Mario. And many thanks for picking up the hospital bills. I really appreciate that."

"I try to treat you guys right. I'm glad you dropped by, there's a few things I'd like to talk to you about. But what is it you want?"

"I know you're busy planning the show for tomorrow, but there is something important to me, and I need another favor of you."

"It's not about one of those pretty girls I've seen you with."

"No, I've managed to handle that situation."

"I wish all the staff could. That incident with Fran was very embarrassing, and even worse, he couldn't work today when we especially needed him. If stories like that get around the trade, our reputation will be ruined. We'll be just another wild resort."

"I don't know what happened, but I heard that Fran caused an ugly scene when his various girlfriends started fighting."

"You're right, and I will not have that happening again in tent city."

"Mario, I have a chance to make a tremendous investment."

"That's very interesting. A young man should always keep his eyes open for a good opportunity. Just what is this investment?"

"I have a chance to buy a car for an excellent price."

"Claxton, you know I was in the car business before I got into resorts. Sometimes what seems great about a car is only your view, not that of the next buyer."

"This car is one that I can enjoy, drive home, and later sell for a profit."

"It's not one of those funeral cars like Jake bought, is it? Those old Packards and Cadillacs are expensive to keep up. Anyway, you will always be able to buy them for a song. You couldn't give me one of them."

"No, it's not one of those. It's a 1939 Mercury convertible."

"How much will it cost?"

"They want three hundred dollars cash by Monday."

"That's a lot of money for an old car. How do you know it's worth it?"

"I told Bones in the kitchen that I had bought it for three hundred, and he immediately offered me four hundred for it."

"Now that's good thinking. Rather than drive it home, you should sell it to Bones and use the hundred profit for your train fare back home."

"Will you advance my salary for this month and any bonus I may get so I can buy the car?"

"Let me think about that for a minute. First, let's talk about tomorrow's show. I haven't seen you at any of the rehearsals. I know it's because you've been sick, but I want you to know that we need you in the show. You had a rough time in the hospital, and I'm sorry about that, but we have problems you can help us with."

"Mario, you know I've made every effort to do each job the best I could."

"You've done a fine job this summer under some difficult circumstances, but I'm a little disappointed that you haven't shown more interest in our Civil War battle. The tennis match was a real success for the program. We've had more people playing tennis this year than ever before, and that definitely gives us a good reputation."

"It's been a good experience for me. At first I was completely lost with all the girls because most of them had never played at all, but even so, they really had enthusiasm."

"The square dance program was the best ever. We all knew that Stanley went out of his way to embarrass you, but you came through like a seasoned showman and won the audience."

"We can credit my partner for that. Bonnie kept me going when I was ready to quit dancing and knock the hell out of him."

"Well, you put one good screwing to the waiters back in June with the shower thing."

"How did you know about that?"

"I know about most things that happen here. Sometimes it takes awhile, but I finally learn about it. For example, I didn't know until last week you had used my car with that French girl —what's her name?"

"Yvonne. Oh my . . . anything else you know?"

"Oh yes, we were afraid you wouldn't survive the romance with Jean, but I've seen these situations before, and they all seem to work out somehow."

"I think I'm much wiser about women after this summer."

"Don't count on that too much. One summer at Handover won't prepare you for a lifetime of dealing with women. I've lived a lot longer than you and I'm still looking for that secret."

"I'll remember that."

"Well, Claxton, we have got to do our show tomorrow, and we need you. J.T. told me about your family experience during the Civil War, and it was moving."

"I know it's just a show, but I wouldn't be comfortable in a Yankee uniform even if you paid me."

"Would three hundred dollars make you comfortable?"

"Not in a Yankee uniform."

"That settles it. You got the three hundred, and you'll be wearing a Confederate uniform."

"I thought you only needed Yankees."

"We can get enough of them from the guests, but more important, we need some people who can be responsible in dangerous situations. And I admire your honesty."

"How dangerous do you mean?"

"Just wait until the rehearsal and you'll see."

Sunday started early for the staff. Breakfast would be the hardest meal to serve of the Labor Day weekend. For most of the guests it was still Saturday night as they came from parked cars in the pine grove or from the Carriage Room where they had passed out earlier. The buses for early Mass were filled by 8 o'clock and left promptly even though many of the passengers were still hung over. I often wondered how some of them managed to get up from kneeling at Mass.

Starting with the happy hour on Saturday, everyone seemed to go berserk. They were all determined to capture the last bit of summer fun, some by reality but most by excessive intoxication.

The Saturday night barbecue in the pine grove started out as a good-humored affair with hungry people enjoying good food. It ended in a food-throwing mess that wasted more food than was eaten. The crazies outnumbered the sane people, so it was impossible to control them.

Tally-Ho was like a zoo. There were so many people that dancing was impossible. Mario had tried to keep the gate crashers out by having mounted horses patrol the fences and gates, but even this was ineffective. The gate crashers had gathered and advanced in large numbers; there were so many of them that security could not stem the tide. But there was one positive effect: as a result of the crashers, many girls who would have been alone ended up with a date. Through all this confusion, Ann and I spent a quiet evening at a movie and then driving around the countryside.

Fortunately for the staff, they had eaten before the Sunday buffet. Many of the staff had missed their dinner Saturday night because of the drunken brawl. Murphy had made sandwiches for them later, but there wasn't enough for everyone. On Sunday the food ran out again, so the drunks at the end of the line began to throw the leftovers that were served to them. I could never understand how people could get so drunk by dinner time, especially those who had gone to church.

Mario was continuously on the public address system announcing the "mock Battle of Bull Run." I don't recall who actually won the battle, but today for sure it was going to be won by the South.

"Attention, y'all. At 7 o'clock in the north pasture, the Cavaliers from Manassas, Virginia, the Handover staff, and guests will reenact the Battle of Bull Run. The Cavaliers are a historical minded group of citizens who have studied the battles of the War Between the States and have reproduced them throughout the nation, and are directed and will be led here by Colonel Robert Byrd from Manassas, Virginia. The battle will open with a heavy artillery exchange and a charge by the Yankee infantry as the Confederates retreat to the hills. The day will be saved by the Confederate calvary who attack from the east flank and rout the Yankees. There are a few surprises, and we won't tell you what those are . . . you'll have to see the show!"

By the time the actors had taken their places, the bank of the road by the pasture was covered with guests. Most of them had drinks in hand and several more inside them. This show attracted far more people than the aborted air show back in June. One reason was that the Virginia people had become well known, and somewhat unpopular, having raised hell in the resort for two days. At times I think some of the guests hoped that the ammunition would be live and maybe kill off the Virginians, who had been a pain in the ass for everyone.

It didn't take long for me to realize what Mario meant by needing responsible people for the show. The cannons and powder were real, but most of the warriors were drunk. We Confederates had three cannon dug in on the high part of the ridge and were to fire as fast as we could load them. I knew nothing about loading cannons, and was afraid they might explode each time they were fired, but the badly inebriated crew (one Virginian and two guests) acted as if it were old stuff to them. The Virginian had shown us how much powder to use with each load, but these guys could hardly find the cannon, much less measure the powder. They had taken the top off the powder keg so they could scoop it up more quickly. This also caught my attention because powder was being spread in every direction.

The big crowd over the weekend had used a lot of water, making the septic tank drain field overflow even more than usual. Rand and I had worked in it the first two weeks we were here, and the situation seemed to have worsened during the summer. The rainy season had made a swamp of the lower pasture, and the septic tank lines had drained into it. The plan was for the Rebel infantry to retreat up the hill, but between them and the hill lay a foot-deep swamp of raw sewage.

At exactly 7 o'clock the cannons started to fire, one round per minute. My job was to take the long rod with the flat end and clean out everything left in the barrel from each firing. One of the drunk guests then poured in the powder, another packed cotton down the barrel, and the gun captain lit the fuse.

The Rebels were in trenches about halfway down the pasture, and the Yankees were advancing from the north road. As we were firing, the Yankee infantry, led by its Calvary, overran the Rebels and hand-to-hand fighting was supposed to take place. The Yankee ranks were made up of staff members and guests who were only interested in the free beer and ten dollars pay. I never understood where they got all the guys for the Yankee calvary, but Denny and Tex were the only ones I recognized. As the Rebels retreated across the sewage-filled swamp with the Yankee calvary in pursuit, the mock battle became a real comedy.

Guys from both sides were bogged up to their knees in mud and raw sewage. Some fell down and were covered with the mess. The acting ended and the fight for survival began. The chemicals had controlled the foul odor most of the summer, but the churning of the water released its full stench. I remembered the smell of the paper mills in Savannah and the rotten-egg odor of hydrogen sulfide in chemistry classes, but this was far worse than either of them.

The most comic scene of all was the Yankee calvary, with Denny at the lead, charging into the swamp. The horses had more sense than the infantry, for they refused to cross. Denny forced his horse to the middle before the horse's front legs buckled and he sent Denny sprawling face down into the sewage. If ever a horse had the last laugh, this had to be his shining moment of revenge on Denny.

The crowd on the bank thought this was the climax of the show, but the biggest surprise was yet to come. The Rebel calvary had been held in reserve in the woods east of the battlefield. Cutting loose with their Rebel yells, they attacked the Yankees on their defenseless flank. Mario, dressed in his finest Confederate gray uniform, led the charge, riding his faithful white stallion, Traveler. The calvary was the star of the show, and was made up of Mario and the Virginians, who were excellent riders. Out across the pasture they came with sabers drawn, hoofs pounding the earth, in full attack on the surprised Yankees.

The attack had only been rehearsed on paper, of course, so Mario and his calvary knew nothing of the fifty-yard wide swamp of raw sewage that lay in front of the hill. The fight for survival in the mud flat, or more accurately the sewage flat, was misinterpreted by Mario and the calvary as fierce hand-to-hand combat, and their chance to save the day had come. What a moment of glory flashed through Mario's mind. Everything is working out perfectly—the crowd is roaring, the cannons are firing, the show is a great success.

Down the slopes in full glory, sabers raised and voices at full Rebel yell, came the heroes of the day. The crowd on the bank cheered and clapped as the calvary horses slipped and fell in the mud, sometimes on their riders and sometimes on infantrymen. By accident or carelessness, someone had spilled a line of powder on the ground that led to the powder keg. Our captain ordered us to fire on the retreating Yankees as the plan had directed. A spark from our round set off the powder on the ground, and in seconds three huge explosions followed in rapid succession.

The crowd was ecstatic, never expecting the mock battle to be so realistic. They cheered and clapped and screamed with excitement—the explosion had been a climax beyond their expectations. With that finale, Mario's reputation as a showman reached new heights.

The first victims to be taken to the hospital were those burned in the explosion. Next were those bruised when hit by horses or cut by sabers. By some miracle the injuries were surprisingly few. The most severe were those close to the powder kegs, but their injuries were not as bad as first appeared. They had minor burns and their hair was singed, but nothing overly serious.

The battlefield scene was complete when the first aid center got into operation. The soft mud, water, and sewage actually provided a cushioning effect that kept many injuries from being worse, but minor cuts and bruises were numerous. Amazingly, none of the horses were hurt to any extent. The Virginia Cavaliers would probably do this show again, but one thing was certain: they would all have to clean and mend their uniforms before the next performance.

Chapter Fifteen

❀ *End of the Summer*

Our Battle of Bull run was over, but for Mario
the show went on:

"Attention guests. Rex Robinson and his band will
be playing in the Tally-Ho beginning at 9 o'clock until 2:00.
The Stompers will play in the Carriage Room from 2:00
until 4:00 a.m. Afterwards, if you like, you can enjoy a
breakfast on your own at one of the all-night places in
town."

For the Labor Day weekend guests, it was two nights
down and one more to go. If you don't score tonight,
ladies, it's back to the City and your dull job for another
year. But the last night is always the best . . . somewhere
in there, somebody wants me. For Mario and the older
staff, it was another season ending; for me it was a new era
beginning. I had a premonition that life would never again
be a straightforward and as frequently pleasurable as here at
the resort this summer..

When I found Ann, she was in tears with fear that I
had been hurt. After all the confusion ended, we had
several drinks and went to her room. It had been a long
summer and I was ready to go home, but how could this last
night have been more perfect? At the very end of the
summer, Handover had lived up to its reputation.

The early morning sunrise from the Mansion back steps offered a poignant view—not as beautiful as the front entrance with its splendor of October Mountain, but a view much more realistic. From that back balcony I could see the tents, the tennis courts, the pine grove, and the stables. I didn't realize that this would really be my last look or how much my life would change. What a beautiful night it had been with Ann. She gave me every pleasure I ever dreamed of, and I had learned over the summer how to please a woman. The night in her room was my first experience of real lovemaking.

After breakfast Ann signed over the title to the car, and I drove her to the bus station.

"Did you have any trouble getting the money from Mario?"

"He was so thankful that no one was seriously hurt and so elated with the crowd reaction that he would have given me twice the amount."

"You know what happened to Frances in this car?"

"I hope it didn't happen to you in room 207."

"Based on my time of the month, it would have been another miracle of biology if it did."

"I'm aware of that, but if it had been any better I couldn't have stood it."

"Will you be back next summer?"

"I hope so, but it looks like some of us will be in the Army."

Ann left on the bus at noon, and I barely got back in time for lunch and our last staff meeting.

"Hi, gang."

"Hi, Mario."

"Well, we made it. I knew we would, but I think we all had a little scare yesterday. There are no announcements; only one brief speech. You have been a grand bunch to work with—the best staff ever. Any time you want to come back, there will always be a place for you. We have the bonuses for you in the office, and drinks for everyone in the library."

J.T. and I had cleaned up the tent and packed everything in the convertible by 5 o'clock. After dinner there was a lot of hugging, kissing goodbye, and a few tears. Some staff didn't want to go and leave the summer romance that had developed. Although they promised to write and see each other, they soon learned that some things are best left behind. We put the top down and drove around the Mansion circle for the last time. The lobby was empty, and all the cars were gone from the pine grove. It was like leaving school again, with all the buildings deserted.

"Did you really get all you wanted?" I asked J.T.

"For the first two months I didn't get anything; then like magic, more than I could take care of. Would you believe I had a different girl on Friday, Saturday, and Sunday?"

"Do you remember that night you brought that married gal to the tent, and I was in my bunk?"

"Do I! She really pissed me off that night, but boy did she make up for it later. How about you? Get all you wanted?"

"I got close most of the time but didn't score a hundred percent."

"Me either."

"I learned that you can never predict what's in store for you," I said.

"Guess we all did."

"Coming back next year, J.T.?"

"Mario sure seems to want us back, didn't he?"

"Sure does. Think we could get waiter jobs?"

"I'd like the money, Clax, but I'm not sure I could work with those bastards."

"When you become one of them, you'll learn to love them. For the money they make, I could even learn to like Stanley."

"I'll be back, regardless," J.T. said.

"Me too."

"That's what you say now, Clax, but once you get back to school with this car, you'll forget about Handover."

"The hell I will. Do you forget about mealtime? I've had a romantic feast here, compared to school."

"Do you think the girls back at school will look as good as some of the ones here?"

"Not for the first month, anyway. Then, who knows?"

~ The golden, beautiful days
  Between youth and manhood
  Between college boys and college men
    Between soldiers of fortune and
    statistics
    of war
  Where did they go?
~ In the 50s from the South
  Came young men to seek
  Excitement, pleasure and love
  In New England, a land of summer
    resorts
  Filled with girls seeking
    Excitement, pleasure, love, and
    marriage.
~ The golden beautiful days
  Short in number as they were
  Filled the dreams of the young men
  And the hopes of the girls
  But all ended too soon
  For the world, time and life,
  Could not wait.